The Easy Essay Handbook

A Writing Guide for Today's Students

JANE E. LEE

LINDY A. FERGUSON

The University of Michigan Press
Ann Arbor

ISBN 0-472-08989-7

Published in the United States of America by
The University of Michigan Press
Typeset by Sans Serif Inc.
Manufactured in the United States of America

2007 2006 2005 2004   4 3 2 1

Acknowledgments

We would like to thank Kelly Sippell and the University of Michigan Press for believing in this book and encouraging our work. Thanks also to Whitney St. Germain for her careful editing help. Finally, we extend our appreciation to the following students who graciously allowed us to include some of their essays in this book: Tomohiro Amemiya, Onur Efendioglu, Chihiro Fujimori, Chiho Fujioka, Mari Murakami, and Miwa Ohashi, and of course to Mika A. Miller, who helped recruit these willing students. Without their cooperation and the efforts of all the other students who have shared their writing with us through the years, this book could not exist.

This book is a result of peaceful relations among nations through-out the world whose citizens have been able to become friends and learn from their global neighbors. We dedicate this book to a re-newed commitment to the continuation and expansion of a co-operative world community.

Contents

Unit 6.   Sample Student Essays   143

To the Student

As you probably know, beginning in 2005, high-stakes tests such as the SAT® and the TOEFL® will require you to write an essay. Applications to colleges or universities also require personal essays or essay-type entrance exams. If you are accepted, the college or university will then require you to write another essay in order to place you in the appropriate English class. Once you are in classes, both English and otherwise, you will be asked to write still more essays, sometimes for an assignment, and sometimes as an essay question on a class test. Perhaps your essay-writing skills have not been fully developed yet, or perhaps you just need to build some confidence about your writing.

You may be thinking, "Help! I know I'm not ready for all that writing. What can I do to prepare myself?" The answers are in this book, which has been designed to help you develop good essay-writing skills by breaking down the whole essay-writing process into simple steps.

Maybe you would like a basic review of paragraph writing and a reminder of the similarities between a basic paragraph and an essay with many paragraphs. Here is where **Unit 1: Paragraph Review** will refresh your memory.

For some people, the biggest problem in getting started is deciding on an appropriate topic for an essay assignment. **Unit 2: Generating Ideas** will show you how to help yourself think of many possible topics for every kind of essay.

After you review these first two units, it is helpful to see how everything fits together. **Unit 3: An Essay Plan from Topic to Final Draft** follows one essay completely through the process of topic selection to a final copy of the essay.

Of course, you will need to match each of your essays to specific assignments. In **Unit 4: Examining Seven Types of Essays,** you can look closely at the seven main essay types: narrative, process, classification, comparison/contrast, cause and effect, persuasion, and definition. Each of these essay types is completely organized for you. First, there is an explanation of the purpose and characteristics of the essay type; next is a model essay with follow-up questions and an individual checklist to reinforce your understanding of each particular essay type.

Included in each of these individual essay sections you will also find different exercises for common writing problems. In addition, if you need help with common grammar problems, you can look at **Unit 5: Mechanics Review.**

Sometimes in individual class situations, an instructor might ask you to read another student's essay in order to help both you and the student who wrote the essay with specific writing problems. The **Peer Feedback Form** and additional peer review questions, found in every section of Unit 4, will show you how to do this.

Finally, if you want to see how other students have done with similar essay assignments, you can check out **Unit 6: Sample Student Essays.** Here, you will find two written drafts, the original and a revised copy, for each essay type.

We think that your question, "What can I do to prepare myself?" is answered in this book. Writing an essay does not have to be an unpleasant, difficult task once you see that it follows a simple process with specific steps from its beginning to its end. After you use *The Easy Essay Handbook,* we know you will decide that essay writing can be quite painless. Perhaps you will even decide that it is rewarding and fun to be able to express your own thoughts for other people to read, learn, be persuaded by, and enjoy.

To the Teacher

Congratulations! You have chosen a practical handbook that will help you instill strong beginning essay-writing skills in your students. Here are some clear, brief (yes, we promise) answers to your questions about the theory behind this *Handbook* and the target students that would best benefit from its use. These answers are followed by a guide to show how you can use this book most effectively to maximize student potential.

Is This Another Five-Paragraph Essay Textbook?

Absolutely not! This is a *Handbook* for students, and it never restricts the student to writing only five paragraphs. We have found from our experience with native and non-native English-speaking beginning writers (from middle school to graduate school) that the basic idea of the multiparagraph essay has to be introduced. The format serves as a springboard for writers just learning how to organize their ideas and convey a specific message. The five-paragraph format is often criticized for stifling student creativity and stylistic development because its writers get bogged down on format. As composition teachers with more than 20 years of experience, we have witnessed just the opposite. With a visual concept and a structured format of how to organize their thoughts, new essay writers can finally put their thoughts on paper. Left to pull ideas out of the air, they would fail to see the relationships that exist among their ideas and, in some cases, decide they have no ideas to write about. The basic foundation of a multiparagraph format gives students a safety zone in which to choose among ideas, show relationships between them, and begin to feel that writing an essay is a manageable task. This format facilitates successful writing experiences for the new, often hesitant and timid, writer. Each unit in the *Handbook* provides a positive experience through which students, new to writing, can build confidence and linguistic skills to write comfortably.

What Kind of Student Could Benefit from This Book?

We have personally used the lessons and format described in this book with both *native and non-native English speaking high school and college-level students*. Those students who are increasingly encountering situations in which they are required to *write an actual essay for academic or professional purposes* will feel the true need for the practical exercise the *Handbook* offers. These students have some basic knowledge of the paragraph concept—a set of sentences in a group about a specific topic—but beyond that point, the student needs the *Handbook* to figure out what to do next. Oftentimes, beginning native and non-native English-speaking *students are overwhelmed with the essay-writing assignment* and feel as if they have failed before they have even begun. (For some non-native English-speaking students, the concept of an *essay* is defined entirely differently in their native languages, and for others, it is altogether non-existent.) *The Easy Essay Handbook* user learns the basic rules in organization and written presentation to write an effective, coherent essay with a clear message. The next goal, beyond this text, is for the student to begin to play with the essay, making it his or her own.

How Were the Essay Models Chosen?

The models in Units 1–4 are a *combination of student/teacher-directed essays*, and some have been edited or modified to fit a desired objective. The topics of the essays are subjects we know that students are already familiar with or could easily research. The levels of different writers are reflected in these essays. The goal of this *Handbook* is to show that even beginning writers can write effective essays. For more skilled writers, there are essay models with more complex sentence structure and intermediate to advanced vocabulary. The essays in Unit 6 were all written by *students preparing for community college*.

Can the *Handbook* Be Used in a Multilevel Class?

Yes. It is not necessary to use the units in the order in which they appear in the text. You can break down the units and use parts of them together in a lesson to address a range of student needs. In addition, because the book provides a variety of exercises as well as checklists and a Peer Feedback Form, you could easily divide the class into work centers or teams to complete different writing activities simultaneously. For students who quickly get comfortable with the suggested format, encourage them to add stylistic elements, elaborate, reorganize ideas, alter the format, and create a personalized essay form. This is the next goal for the successful, confident, developing writer. The text allows students to advance at a personalized pace.

A Guide for the Teacher

We have chosen to call this book a *handbook* because its contents are concentrated on the development and improvement of very practical writing skills. *The Easy Essay Handbook* will show students that they can produce effective essays for any class assignment, essay test, or application. Furthermore, they will learn that essay writing does not have to be a frustrating, overwhelming task if it is broken into several concrete, manageable steps.

We also believe that this text can make essay instruction more effective and essay marking less burdensome for teachers. Following are explanations and suggestions for using the different sections of *The Easy Essay Handbook*.

UNIT 1: PARAGRAPH REVIEW

We have created *The Easy Essay Handbook* assuming that the students who use it have already had at least some fundamental experience with independent paragraph writing. The first part of this unit (1.1 Parts of a Paragraph) should be used as a quick reminder about the elements of a basic independent paragraph. Students can then benefit by examining the second part of this unit (1.2 Expanding the Independent Paragraph to an Essay) as it shows a direct relationship from independent paragraphs to essay paragraphs by developing one of the independent paragraphs from Part 1.1 into a complete essay.

Helpful Hint

Although it is not stated directly in Unit 1, teachers might also point out to students that the same topic of the independent paragraphs, smoking cigarettes, can be written with different purposes, just as an essay can be. For example, in the first independent paragraph the purpose is persuasion, in the second it is narration, and in the third cause and effect. (If this information is too overwhelming in the beginning, teachers can refer to it in later writing assignments.)

UNIT 2: GENERATING IDEAS

Unit 2 offers specific ways to help writers choose individual topics, especially by encouraging them to ask themselves or each other questions. The questions deal with firsthand experience and could apply to any of the different essay types presented in this book. We have used these questions because for most inexperienced essay writers, it is relatively easy to discover suitable topics when they think about their own experiences. There is also a list of very general topics that students may already know something about or could research. This chapter also shows writing students how to narrow a topic in order to maintain a clear focus in their essays. They will see that they must be prepared to supply sufficient examples and details for their chosen topic. If students know that the teacher is going to ask, "Why?" and "What proof will you give as examples?" they will learn that they need to consider answers to those questions as they choose their topics.

Unit 2 is designed to help students think of topics for their writing assignments, but we know from experience that teachers always need to have a clear writing goal in mind before talking to the class about which topic to use. When the assignment is too open-ended, such as "Write about whatever you want" or "Choose a topic from this list" without further direction, there will usually be two undesirable results, one for the students and one for the teacher. Many students will feel confused and waste valuable writing time trying to figure out exactly what is expected of them. Once they hand in their papers, the teacher will have to decide how to evaluate the often vague and sometimes completely unacceptable results.

Helpful Hint

Checking the essay topics and lists of subtopics with students before they actually begin to write will greatly reduce later misunderstandings and/or frustration for the students and for the teacher. Sometimes it is helpful to ask students to choose three topics related to an essay assignment and to write as many subtopics as they can for each potential topic. When they list these topics, it usually becomes apparent to them that one of the topics will be easier to develop by example than the others, so it is most likely their best choice.

UNIT 3: AN ESSAY PLAN FROM TOPIC TO FINAL DRAFT

This unit breaks down the essay-writing process from beginning to end with an example essay. The special importance of Unit 3 is that it shows students that they can greatly improve their writing if they concentrate on only one major writing skill at a time. They also learn that good writing requires rewriting. The process begins with topic selection and a rough outline or a list of subtopic examples to be used in the essay. (See Unit 2.) After that, there is a fully written draft that concentrates only on the content of the essay to ensure that it will contain adequate information. Then a second written draft addresses essay organization to emphasize the importance of the flow of an essay from introductory paragraph through body paragraphs to the concluding paragraph. Finally, the third draft is written with attention to possible grammatical or spelling errors. A main objective in the order of steps in this process is to emphasize to teachers as well as to students that the "mechanics" of the writing are never as important as the actual content and organizational flow that make the essay enjoyable to read. In addition, teachers and students usually discover that many writing errors have been corrected by the time the writer gets to the final draft. The system from this unit can be used in any writing class for any essay assignment.

Helpful Hint

Teachers benefit in following each step in this process by being able to pinpoint progress and problems very specifically as they occur and to help students keep their writing on track. In addition, requiring students to show each step in the essay process greatly discourages the temptation of plagiarism, a most unpleasant issue that is much easier to prevent than to confront when a student hands in a suspiciously polished final essay that looks nothing like his or her usual class work.

REMEMBER WHEN MARKING STUDENT WRITING

It is easy for teachers to point out mechanical errors, but it is not as useful for developing writers as when teachers make specific comments (positive wherever possible) about the contents of the student writing.

It is not necessary to grade lower-level writers' essays to the detailed extent that a more skilled writer's essay may require. In fact, it is counter-productive to do so. It is recommended that teachers choose a few areas of difficulty for each student and address those when correcting the writing. The purpose of marking an essay is to note the writer's progress. When the teacher makes too many corrections, it is no longer the student's essay.

UNIT 4: EXAMINING SEVEN TYPES OF ESSAYS

Unit 4 contains a wealth of material that can be used in many different writing assignments. The core of the unit is the presentation of seven different essay types. The essay types represent the most common kinds of essays that students might be assigned, whether for English and other academic classes, essay questions on tests, or essays written for applications. We have chosen the order of the essays in what we consider to range from the easiest to the most difficult. While it is not essential to adhere to the essay order in this unit, we strongly recommend that developing writers start with the narrative essay because it is usually the easiest to write. Each essay type is represented by one model essay except for the section on comparison/contrast essays. There we have included two different examples partially because this is a very common type of essay, especially on academic essay tests, and because we want to show two different approaches to the organization of the material.

Each essay type is first explained in reference to its specific purpose and characteristics. Following the actual essay model is a set of questions designed to help students further understand the specific purpose and characteristics through careful study of that particular model essay.

Included after each model essay is a very detailed checklist that covers three different areas for each essay type. These checklists are for students and teachers to use with the essays that the students will eventually write; they may be reproduced for classroom use. First, there are very specific questions about the content of the essay to reinforce the purpose of any individual essay type. The second area covers organization, again with specific questions for that essay type. The third part is called mechanics, and this section is the same on the checklist for each type of essay. The mechanics part details the most common weaknesses of beginning writers, primarily in terms of mistakes in grammar.

Each model essay section also has a segment called *Got It!* with exercises designed to address common writing problems. Following the Narrative Essay model is an exercise focused on introductory and concluding paragraphs. Since all essays will need introductory and concluding paragraphs, this *Got It!* can be applied to other essay types as well. In fact, each *Got It!* exercise relates directly to the type of model it follows, but (with the exception of the very specific exercise in the Comparison/Contrast section) any or all of these exercises can be used in connection with any or all of the other models. For example, if students are having difficulty in writing specific examples, they should be directed to the *Got It!* following the Classification Essay in 4.3 where they are guided to create "word pictures" that can be applied to any type of essay.

Finally, each model essay section has a Peer Feedback Form. If teachers are introducing the concept of examining other students' writing, it is important to refer first to the explanation about peer feedback and the complete Peer Feedback Form, both of which follow the Narrative Essay, the first model essay in this unit. There are shorter feedback forms following all the other model essays; all are reproducible for classroom use. Unlike the checklists, these forms are not restricted to the model essay that they follow, so they can be used by themselves or in any combination.

Helpful Hint

Yes, we know the checklists are extremely itemized, but we have a purpose in breaking them down into such excruciating detail. We believe that such details help beginning writers stay focused on their goal. After students have more writing experience, obviously the checklists can be modified.

The checklists can also be used to grade different areas of the final essay. Students who provide outstanding content through their use of clear examples, vivid language, and "word pictures" but who are spelling-challenged in the same essay can be rewarded with the highest mark for content and a much lower one for mechanics to encourage more careful proofreading in the future. (Some students can create essays that you really enjoy reading, but they make several grammatical errors. If the errors do not impede your understanding of the essays, we believe that these writers show a lot more promise than one who makes zero errors in mechanics but whose content totally lacks imagination.) The organization portion is generally manageable by most students after one or two essay efforts, but obviously, the flow of any essay is always important.

A SPECIAL CHECKLIST BONUS FOR TEACHERS
Maintaining your own copies of the checklists is extremely useful in gauging students' improvement in specific content, organization, and mechanics areas from one essay to the next.

UNIT 5: MECHANICS REVIEW

Mechanics in the title refers to common grammatical errors, so the exercises in this section should be used for students who make the specific errors covered in the exercises. Probably the most common grammatical errors will be found in students' incomplete and/or run-on sentences, so we have provided several exercises to address those problems. Other points in Unit 5 will apply to individual students, but ESL students especially might benefit from all of the grammar review in this unit.

Helpful Hint

This text is in no way intended to be a grammar book. For students with serious English grammar deficiency, the exercises in this section are only supplements to a more thorough study of grammar.

UNIT 6: SAMPLE STUDENT ESSAYS

The sample essays in Unit 6 were all written by ESL students who were preparing to enter community college. Their essays have been included to show how a checklist completed between two different drafts of the same essay was used to show the writer precisely how to improve the essay. There is one sample student essay for each essay type, and the checklists that are used are the same checklists as those in the individual essay sections.

Helpful Hint

The essays in this section are obviously less developed than the model essays in Unit 4, but especially for beginning essay writers, they can provide encouragement by demonstrating that it is possible for all students to improve their writing, no matter what their present skills might be.

Paragraph Review

1.1 Parts of a Paragraph

A paragraph is a group of related sentences. Sometimes a paragraph is a complete unit by itself, but more often it is part of an essay. Before you learn to write essays with many body paragraphs, it is a good idea to review how to write independent paragraphs. The paragraph that stands alone contains more or less the same essential parts as a complete essay: it needs a beginning, a middle, and an ending. For independent paragraph writing, the beginning is called the **topic sentence,** the middle is called the **body,** and the ending is called the **concluding sentence.**

EXAMPLE PARAGRAPH 1

To begin, the writer needs a topic sentence. A proper topic sentence tells the reader both what the paragraph will be about and what the writer will prove or discuss about that topic.

Example topic sentence 1:

Smoking cigarettes can produce several unpleasant results.

The topic sentence states that the writer will show unpleasant results of smoking. Here are some possible negative effects that the writer could write about.

- **diseases**
- **changes in appearance**
- **smells**

After the writer has written these examples in the form of complete sentences with specific details, he or she needs to add a concluding sentence. The concluding sentence shows readers that he or she has completed all examples and that there is no more new material. A conclusion is usually a restatement of the topic sentence, but in different words. An example concluding sentence for this paragraph follows.

> **It might be a difficult choice, but smokers need to decide if any or all of these negative effects are worth any pleasure they may get from smoking.**

The final paragraph might look like this:

> **Smoking cigarettes can produce several unpleasant results.** Scientists have found that cigarette smokers have a high risk of contracting lung or throat cancer, especially if they smoke for many years. Emphysema, a really gruesome way of death, is another lung disorder often related to smoking. Heart disease is still another potential result of smoking as are strokes, which are the result of a blocked or broken blood vessel and which can cause death or paralysis. If these diseases aren't horrible enough, smokers might want to think about their appearance. As the smoke curls up from their lips, their eyes often squint to keep the smoke out. Years of this repeated action might cause deep wrinkles that will make smokers look much older than their actual ages. Finally, in consideration of other people, smokers can be unpleasant companions to live with when their breath, hair, and clothes grab onto the smell of the smoke and won't let go without thorough teeth brushing, hair shampooing, and/or clothes laundering. **It might be a difficult choice, but smokers need to de-**

cide if all or any of these negative effects are worth any pleasure they may get from smoking cigarettes.

EXAMPLE PARAGRAPH 2

Here is a different topic sentence about smoking cigarettes.

For a ten-year-old, smoking cigarettes can cost more than just money.

The topic is still smoking cigarettes, but this writer will explain what the additional costs were for him when he was ten years old. Here is a list of his "costs."

- **grounded**
- **no television**
- **washing all family dishes**

After writing the examples as detailed sentences, the writer needs to add a concluding sentence.

The final paragraph might look like this:

For a ten-year-old, smoking cigarettes can cost more than just money.

Actually, the price of the cigarettes was pretty cheap because my friend's brother let us have two for only one dollar apiece. The real paying part started after my dad caught us smoking when he came home early from work and heard the radio playing loudly behind the garage. "Young man," he said, "I hope that smoking with your friend helps you remember him because you won't see each other, or any other friends again for two weeks." Being grounded was only Step One in my dad's plan because after my friend left and we went inside, Dad added "zero television" to my punishment, and yes, "zero" included shows I wouldn't, in all honesty, ever even want to watch. When my mom learned about the incident, she broke out in a huge smile as she realized that my smoking had provided her with a live-in slave. She told me that I would wash all the dishes for two weeks. This was worse than it sounds because it was summertime, and my sisters and I had been eating and drinking whenever we felt like it, just adding to the gigantic piles of dirty glasses and dishes in the sink. **To no one's surprise, long before the two weeks were completed, I had decided that smoking was way too expensive, and so my first cigarette was also my last.**

EXAMPLE PARAGRAPH 3

Here is one more example with the same topic, but with a different purpose.

> **The laws of California might help people who want to quit smoking cigarettes.**

Again the topic is smoking cigarettes, but this time, in the topic sentence, the writer promises to tell the reader about the cigarette-related laws. Thus, the writer needs examples of laws:

- **no smoking inside public buildings**
- **no smoking in restaurants or bars**
- **no cigarette advertising on television or billboards**

After writing the body sentences, the writer needs to add a concluding sentence. The final paragraph might look like this:

> **The laws of California might help people who want to quit smoking cig-arettes.** First, there is no smoking allowed in public buildings, and almost all workplaces must prohibit indoor smoking. Even if smokers don't have a job and therefore don't have a workplace to restrict their smoking, it's certain that they do at least occasionally go to public buildings, which include theaters, shops, super-

markets, indoor shopping malls, and indoor sports arenas. Like the rest of us, smokers enjoy eating out, and anyone who has ever smoked knows that the cigarette that tastes the very best is the one after a satisfying meal. Smokers can forget that delicious "dessert cigarette" unless they are willing to go completely outside the restaurant to stand and smoke. The same outside smoking rule applies to bars and discos. Furthermore, the temptation to smoke may be lessened because of the prohibition of cigarette advertising on television. Smokers won't see those now forbidden cigarette billboards while driving or walking down the streets either. **Whether there is a law that restricts the places of smoking or there is one that forbids the advertising of cigarettes, if you know a smoker who would like to quit, you might suggest a stay in California.**

As you learn to write each type of essay, you will see that the body paragraphs of a multiparagraph essay are very similar to these individual paragraphs. To illustrate the similarities and the slight differences, we return to the first independent paragraph (Example Paragraph 1) and expand it into a multiparagraph essay.

1.2 Expanding the Independent Paragraph to an Essay

First, we will take the topic sentence of the independent paragraph *(Smoking cigarettes can produce several unpleasant results.)* and modify it slightly to create our thesis statement for the essay. While the topic sentence announces to the reader what will be discussed in a paragraph, the thesis statement announces what will be discussed in an essay. The thesis statement will be the last sentence of the introductory paragraph, the last sentence before we begin to support and prove it in the body of the essay.

We begin the essay with some general comments that will *introduce* our topic and lead us into the main point of the entire essay, the **thesis statement.** These general comments plus the thesis statement form the first paragraph, the *introduction* to the essay.

The sample introductory paragraph, with the thesis statement at the end:

Cigarette smoking has been a popular activity for many people for many years. Some smokers claim that smoking cigarettes provides relaxation, while some other smokers maintain that, for them, cigarette smoking is desirable because it gives them the necessary stimulation to think more clearly and productively. Depending on smokers' wishes at the moment, either relaxation or stimulation can be desirable and enjoyable. **The problem is that cigarette smoking can also produce unpleasant results for the smoker and for others as well.**

Through the thesis statement, we (as writers) have promised to talk about unpleasant results, so for each of the body paragraphs, we will take one of the main points from the independent paragraph (see page 2) and use it as the topic sentence for the first body paragraph. Next, we elaborate with details.

Probably the most obvious undesirable result of smoking is a serious disease. After many years of research, scientists have concluded that throat and lung cancers are sometimes the result of smoking cigarettes, especially if people have been smoking for many years. Other lung diseases that have been related to cigarette smoking are chronic bronchitis and emphysema. If smokers have chronic bronchitis, they often suffer from painful coughing spasms. In the advanced stages of emphysema, patients are restricted from an even slightly active life, and they often struggle for every single breath they take. Heart disease, a problem of increased heart rate or abnormal heart rhythms, is also related to smoking. A stroke, the consequence of a blocked or broken blood vessel, can result in death or paralysis, and has been linked to smoking too. To be sure, any one of these physical weaknesses could keep cigarette smokers from living full, active lives.

Now we make a connection from the "disease" paragraph to the next body paragraph with the second main point from the independent paragraph (see page 2).

Although they are not fatal and do not necessarily affect cigarette smokers' lifestyles, smokers' physical appearances can be negatively affected by smoking. When smokers exhale cigarette smoke from their lungs, some of the smoke goes up toward their eyes, causing them to squint. After many years and many cigarettes, this narrowing of the eyes produces wrinkles, particularly the type known as "crow's feet," deep furrows at the outer edges of the eyes which make smokers appear older than they actually are. Other unflattering appearance results are sometimes found on the fingers that typically hold the cigarette and therefore become yellowed, and on smokers' teeth that may also become stained from years of nicotine. Perhaps smokers should accept that they might eventually spend much of their time and money on cosmetic surgery and teeth-whitening procedures to remove these unattractive "scars" of smoking.

Again, we make a connection from the "appearance" paragraph to the next body paragraph with the last main point from the independent paragraph.

Cigarette smokers may say that if they get these diseases or wrinkles, it is their choice, but unfortunately, those around them are also affected by cigarette smoking. There is still some controversy about the physical effects of "second-hand smoke," but anyone who lives with a smoker knows that there are plenty of other annoyances. Inside the living quarters, whether house or apartment, there are almost always used ashtrays, which are unpleasant, especially if they are not emptied or washed often. Even worse than the ashtrays is the smell from the cigarettes. When smokers live with non-smokers, they need to take extra care in keeping their breath, hair, and clothing clean and as free of the tobacco smell as possible. No matter what the relationship between the persons might be, nobody wants to be near someone who reeks of stale tobacco, let alone to kiss this person. In addition, smokers should pay attention to the odor from old closed-in smoke that clings to the furnishings in rooms, especially to curtains and over-stuffed sofas and chairs. Once they face the fact that their smoking is not pleasant to the non-smokers who share their living space, thoughtful smokers will do their cigarette smoking outdoors.

We have finished the body of the essay, so now we need a **concluding sentence.** The concluding paragraph begins by restating the thesis statement, which is followed by a short summary to complete the essay. We can use the concluding sentence from the independent paragraph (see page 2) for our thesis statement.

It might be a difficult choice, but smokers need to decide if any or all of these negative effects are worth any pleasure they may get from smoking. Whether smokers use cigarettes for relaxation or for stimulation, the physical act of smoking is for only a few moments. The consequences to themselves and others, however, can be for a lifetime.

INDEPENDENT PARAGRAPH

Here again is the independent paragraph. It is followed by the complete essay that we have developed from it.

Smoking cigarettes can produce several unpleasant results. Scientists have found that cigarette smokers have a high risk of contracting lung or throat cancer, especially if they smoke for many years. Emphysema, a really gruesome way of death, is another lung disorder often related to smoking. Heart disease is still another potential result of smoking as are strokes, which are the result of a blocked or broken vessel and which can cause death or paralysis. If these diseases aren't horrible enough, smokers might want to think about their appearance. As the smoke curls up from their lips, their eyes often squint to keep the smoke out. Years of this repeated action might cause deep wrinkles that will make smokers look much older than their actual ages. Finally, in consideration of other people, smokers can be unpleasant companions to live with when their breath, hair, and clothes grab onto the smell of the smoke and won't let go without thorough teeth brushing, hair shampooing, and/or clothes laundering. It might be a difficult choice, but smokers need to decide if all or any of these negative effects are worth any pleasure they may get from smoking cigarettes.

ESSAY

INTRO
PARAGRAPH

Cigarette smoking has been a popular activity for many people for many years. Some smokers claim that smoking cigarettes provides relaxation, while some other smokers maintain that, for them, cigarette smoking is desirable because it gives them the necessary stimultion to think more clearly and productively. Depending on smokers' wishes at the moment, either relaxation or stimulation can be desirable and enjoyable. The problem is that cigarette smoking can also produce unpleasant results for the smoker and for others as well.

BODY
PARAGRAPH
#1

Probably the most obvious undesirable result of smoking is a serious disease. After many years of research, scientists have concluded that throat and lung cancers are sometimes the result of smoking cigarettes, especially if people have been smoking for many years. Other lung diseases that have been related to cigarette smoking are chronic bronchitis and emphysema. If smokers have chronic bronchitis, they often suffer from painful coughing spasms. In the advanced stages of emphysema, patients are restricted from an even slightly active life, and they often struggle for every single breath they take. Heart disease, a problem of increased heart rate or abnormal heart rhythms, is also related to smoking. A stroke, the consequence of a blocked or broken blood vessel, can result in death or paralysis, and has been linked to smoking too. To be sure, any one of these physical weaknesses could keep cigarette smokers from living, full active lives.

BODY
PARAGRAPH
#2

Although they are not fatal and do not necessarily affect cigarette smokers' lifestyles, smokers' physical appearances can be negatively affected by smoking. When smokers exhale cigarette smoke from their lungs, some of the smoke goes up toward their eyes, causing them to squint. After many years and many cigarettes, this narrowing of the eyes produces wrinkles, particularly the type known as "crow's feet," deep furrows at the outer edges of the eyes which make smokers appear older than they actually are. Other unflattering appearance results are sometimes found on the fingers that typically hold the cigarette and therefore become yellowed, and on smokers' teeth that may also become stained from years of nicotine. Perhaps smokers should accept that they might eventually spend much of their time and money on cosmetic surgery and teeth-whitening procedures to remove these unattractive "scars" of smoking.

BODY
PARAGRAPH
#3

Cigarette smokers may say that if they get these diseases or wrinkles, it is their choice, but unfortunately, those around them are also affected by cigarette smoking. There is still some controversy about the physical effects of "second-hand smoke," but anyone who lives with a smoker knows that there are plenty of other annoyances. Inside the living quarters, whether house or apartment, there are almost always used ashtrays, which are unpleasant, especially if they are not emptied or washed often. Even worse than the ashtrays is the smell from the cigarettes. When smokers live with non-smokers, they need to take extra care in keeping their breath, hair, and clothing clean and as free of the tobacco smell as possible. No matter what the relationship between the persons might be, nobody wants to be near someone who reeks of stale tobacco, let alone to kiss this person. In addition, smokers should pay attention to the odor from old closed-in smoke that clings to the furnishings in rooms, especially to curtains and over-stuffed sofas and chairs. Once they face the fact that their smoking is not pleasant to the non-smokers who share their living space, thoughtful smokers will do their cigarette smoking outdoors.

CONCLUDING
PARAGRAPH

It might be a difficult choice, but smokers need to decide if any or all of these negative effects are worth any pleasure they may get from smoking. Whether smokers use cigarettes for relaxation or for stimulation, the physical act of smoking is only for a few moments. The consequences to themselves and others, however, can be for a lifetime.

Got It!
Transitions

Transitions are words or phrases that link ideas and help the essay flow smoothly. Transitions show the relationship between ideas and make it easy for the reader to follow the writer's message. They are used to explain emphasis, contrast, comparison, cause and effect, additional ideas, conditions, and concession. Look at some transition words and phrases below.

although	however	nevertheless	unless
if	despite	besides	on the other hand
because of	furthermore	then	in addition
but	yet	while	therefore
so that	in fact	consequently	not to mention
in order to	thus	not only . . . but	due to the fact that
first	providing	and	even if
in contrast	actually	in comparison	as a result

Can you image how confusing some sentences, paragraphs, and essays would be without them? Look at the following sentences.

Our coach has had ten years of experience. He was a star forward on a professional team for thirteen years.

Our basketball coach has had *not only* ten years of coaching experience, *but* also thirteen years as a star forward on a professional team.

In the first example, the reader cannot identitfy why the writer is mentioning the coach's accomplishments. Through the use of **not only . . . but** in the second example, the reader is able to sense the emphasis in the writer's message that the basketball coach has been successful in more than one area.

TRANSITIONS IN A PARAGRAPH

As a writer, you need to use transition words and phrases inside sentences (not all of them!), in paragraphs, and between body paragraphs in an essay. Look at the following paragraph and circle the transitions that best complete the sentences.

The laws of California might help people who want to quit smoking

cigarettes. _____, there is no smoking allowed in public buildings,
　　　　　　　　　1. First/Then

_____ almost all workplaces must prohibit indoor smoking. _____
　　2. and/but　　　　　　　　　　　　　　　　　　　　　　　　3. Despite/Even if

smokers don't have a job and _____ don't have a workplace to
　　　　　　　　　　　　　　　4. therefore/besides

restrict their smoking, it's certain that they do at least occasionally go to public

buildings, which include theaters, shops, supermarkets, indoor shopping malls,

and indoor sports arenas. Like the rest of us, smokers enjoy eating out, and

anyone who has ever smoked knows that the cigarette that tastes the very

best is the one after a satisfying meal. Smokers can forget that delicious

"dessert cigarette" _____ they are willing to go completely
　　　　　　　　5. unless/not to mention

outside the restaurant to stand and smoke. The same outside smoking rule

applies to bars and discos. _____, the temptation to smoke
                                    6. Furthermore/Thus

may be lessened _____ the prohibition of cigarette ad-
                        7. because of/in order to

vertising on television. Smokers won't see those now forbidden cigarette

billboards while driving or walking down the streets either. Whether there is a

law that restricts the places of smoking or there is one that forbids the

advertising of cigarettes, _____ you know a smoker who would like to
                                8. if/not only

quit, you might suggest a stay in California.

TRANSITIONS IN AN ESSAY

In more advanced essay writing, transitional sentences are used between body paragraphs in an essay. They help the reader move clearly from one paragraph's idea to the next while understanding the relationship between the ideas. Look at the set of three body paragraphs below and note the **bolded** words. After you have read the paragraphs, decide how the bolded words connect the ideas in each paragraph.

BODY   Probably the most obvious undesirable result of smoking
PARAGRAPH   is a serious **disease.** After many years of research, scien-
#1   tists have concluded that throat and lung cancers are
              sometimes the result of smoking cigarettes, especially if
              people have been smoking for many years. Other lung dis-
              eases that have been related to cigarette smoking are
              chronic bronchitis and emphysema. If smokers have
              chronic bronchitis, they often suffer from painful coughing
              spasms. In the advanced stages of emphysema, patients
              are restricted from an even slightly active life, and they

often struggle for every single breath they take. Heart disease, a problem of increased heart rate or abnormal heart rhythms, is also related to smoking. A stroke, the consequence of a blocked or broken blood vessel, can result in **death** or paralysis, and has been linked to smoking too. To be sure, any one of these **physical weaknesses** could keep cigarette smokers from living, **full active lives.**

BODY
PARAGRAPH
#2

　　Although they are not **fatal** and do not necessarily affect cigarette smokers' **lifestyles,** smokers' physical appearances can be negatively affected by smoking. When smokers exhale cigarette smoke from their lungs, some of the smoke goes up toward their eyes, causing them to squint. After many years and many cigarettes, this narrowing of the eyes produces wrinkles, particularly the type known as "crow's feet," deep furrows at the outer edges of the eyes which make smokers appear older than they actually are. Other unflattering appearance results are sometimes found on the fingers that typically hold the cigarette and therefore become yellowed, and on smokers' teeth that may also become stained from years of nicotine. Perhaps smokers should accept that they might eventually spend much of their time and money on cosmetic surgery and teeth-whitening procedures to remove these unattractive **"scars" of smoking**.

BODY PARAGRAPH #3

Cigarette smokers may say that if they get these **diseases** or **wrinkles**, it is their choice, but unfortunately, those around them are also affected by cigarette smoking. There is still some controversy about the physical effects of "second-hand smoke," but anyone who lives with a smoker knows that there are plenty of other annoyances. Inside the living quarters, whether house or apartment, there are almost always used ashtrays, which are unpleasant, especially if they are not emptied or washed often. Even worse than the ashtrays is the smell from the cigarettes. When smokers live with non-smokers, they need to take extra care in keeping their breath, hair, and clothing clean and as free of the tobacco smell as possible. No matter what the relationship between the persons might be, nobody wants to be near someone who reeks of stale tobacco, let alone to kiss this person. In addition, smokers should pay attention to the odor from old closed-in smoke that clings to the furnishings in rooms, especially to curtains and over-stuffed sofas and chairs. Once they face the fact that their smoking is not pleasant to the non-smokers who share their living space, thoughtful smokers will do their cigarette smoking outdoors.

Notice that the word *fatal* in the first sentence of BODY PARAGRAPH #2 has the same meaning as the word *death* in BODY PARAGRAPH #1. Also, the word *lifestyles* in BODY PARAGRAPH #2 refers to the phrases *physical weaknesses* and *full active lives* in BODY PARAGRAPH #1.

Next, notice that the word *diseases* in the first sentence of BODY PARA-GRAPH #3 is repeated from BODY PARAGRAPH #1. The word *wrinkles* from

BODY PARAGRAPH #3 refers to the phrase *"scars" of smoking* in BODY PARAGRAPH #2.

death ———————	fatal
physical weaknesses ———————	lifestyles
full active lives ———————	lifestyles
disease ———————	diseases
"scars" of smoking ———————	wrinkles

 ## Your Turn!

Choose three essays from Unit 4 in this text. For each one, find the transition words and phrases that help the overall flow of the writing.

Generating Ideas

2.1 What Can I Write About?

Before you write an essay, you will most likely be given a specific question or a general topic about which to write. From this point, you need to decide what subtopics or details you will use to answer that question or discuss the assigned topic. (A subtopic is a smaller topic related to the main topic you have been given.) For example, if you were given an assignment to write about perfect vacations, subtopics might include a vacation at the beach, a vacation in the mountains, or a vacation at home. Those would be just a few of the possible subtopics you could write about related to the main assigned topic. You may be surprised to know that specific writing ideas can be generated just by letting your mind wander through your own life. All your life you have been accumulating experiences, interacting with different people, going places, and doing activities every day. Your past, your present, and sometimes your future can all be excellent sources of details and subtopics.

You can gather those writing ideas by brainstorming with partners or by asking and answering questions by yourself. Below are general questions that you can ask for any topic you have been assigned. The example assignment we will use here is an assignment to write an essay about a vacation memory. You will see that, for each question, we have inserted the assigned topic in parentheses so that you can ask questions specific to that topic. (You can use these same questions for any assignment, inserting the assigned topic in parentheses as we have done here.)

Asking about Experiences

- What are some of your (vacations) that were/are especially exciting, happy, sad, surprising, disappointing, or frightening?
- Have any of those (vacations) changed your thinking or your life in any important way? How?
- Would you like to relive any of these (vacations) if you could? Which events would you relive?
- Would you like to change any of these (vacation events) if you could? Which ones would you change? How would you change them?
- What are some (vacations) you hope to have in the future?

Asking about People

- Which people (on vacations) have affected your life most strongly?
- Who were/are they: family members, friends, neighbors, teachers, co-workers, bosses, or perhaps strangers that you met only one time?
- Was/Is your interaction with them mostly positive or mostly negative? Why?
- Is there someone that you hope comes into your life in the future? Who? Why?

Asking about Places

- Which (vacation) places bring out strong feelings for you?
- Were/Are these typical (vacation places) or somewhere that you went for a special event?
- What details can you remember about these places?
- Is there somewhere you would really like to go in the future? Where? Why?

Asking about Activities

- Which (vacation) activities in your life have been special?
- Were they hobbies, sports, clubs, games you played, or maybe even work-related activities?
- What is a (vacation) activity that you have never done that you would love to try in the future?

Asking about Material Objects

- Which objects have been special (on your vacation)?
- Were these objects toys from your childhood, gifts from others, things you worked to buy for yourself, or something you found one day?
- Why were/are these things so special to you?
- Have they changed your life in some way?

Another way to generate ideas is to make a list of subjects that interest you and that you already have some knowledge about or that you could easily research. After you make your list, ask yourself what information you have on each subtopic that you could teach or explain to other people.

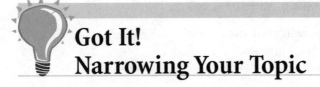

Got It!
Narrowing Your Topic

For this example assignment, a writer was told to write an essay about a personal vacation experience, either a good one or a bad one. Here is a list of words and phrases the writer came up with after just a few minutes.

Step 1: Brainstorm

Good	*Bad*
fun	homesick
swimming	scared
hotel pool	train ride
new friends	strangers
video games	boring town
	movie couldn't see
	cemetery
	pepper
	carsick

The writer's BAD list has many more details, so this will be the main topic of the essay. Next, the student created a brief outline of subtopics to use for an essay about a vacation memory. He had to look at the list and then make an outline to use as a general plan for the essay. Look at his ideas and subtopics below.

Step 2: Outline

SUBJECT: A Vacation Memory from When I Was Nine
SUBTOPIC: Who I Planned to Visit
    Detail 1: same age cousin
    Detail 2: strange feeling
SUBTOPIC: How I Travelled
    Detail 1: first train ride
    Detail 2: carsick feeling
SUBTOPIC: Meeting My Cousin
    Detail 1: big and loud
    Detail 2: asked for gifts
SUBTOPIC: Where to go, what to do
    Detail 1: no swimming pool
    Detail 2: strange movie theater
    Detail 3: stories in cemetery
SUBTOPIC: The Worst Part of the Vacation
    Detail 1: cousin sitting on me.
    Detail 2: black pepper

Now take a look at how the student used this outline to write an essay. Most of the work was already done in the outline.

Everybody knows that going on vacation is supposed to be fun. Something that is supposed to be fun is not at all the same as something that will be fun. I learned the difference during a vacation that was not very fun at all when I was nine years old.

My parents thought my cousin who was my same age and I should get to know each other. She lived in another state, so we had never spent any time together. In fact, the only time we were ever in the same place was when we were babies. I was not really looking forward to leaving my friends to spend time with somebody I didn't even know, but my parents told me that my cousin and I would have fun together.

Part of the fun was supposed to be taking a train for the first time. I guess my parents thought that the movement on a train would not be the same as a car, or else they forgot that I almost always got carsick when I traveled anywhere. I don't know if it's because I was a little nervous and scared, but sure enough, I got that terrible, familiar feeling of being sorry I had eaten lunch before I got on the train. To try to keep myself from feeling any sicker, I started counting all the utility poles I could see from the train window.

The train arrived and I looked around for my stranger cousin. A big, loud girl about my age and her mother came up to me, and while the mother was hugging me and saying, "You look just like your mother did!" the big, loud girl yelled, "Did you bring me anything?" This was not a good beginning to a fun vacation.

The next week was endless. The town where my cousin lived was very small and very boring. It was summertime, and my aunt thought we needed to be outside as much as possible. The swimming pool was closed for repairs, so there was pretty much nothing I really wanted to do. We went to see a free movie, but it was in a building that used to be some kind of store, so we had to sit on uncomfortable folding chairs with big, tall people in front of us so we almost couldn't see anything. The only other place we went that week was to the cemetery. My cousin thought it was really fun to make up stories about the dead people to try to scare me, which wasn't very hard to do.

The very worst part of the week was the pepper incident. I don't really know where she got the idea, but my cousin loved to get me down on the ground to torture me. She was much bigger than I was, so she would just push me over, and then she would sit on me. She had a peppershaker that was filled with black pepper. She would stick the shaker under my nose. First, I would sneeze, and then I cried. I still think about her whenever I smell pepper today.

I was so homesick during that "vacation" that I cried every night after my cousin went to sleep. The only good thing at all was my aunt's sugar cookies. I think she must have had some sort of idea of how miserable I was because every day she let me have as many of those great cookies as I wanted. To me that week was longer than seven days, but now I realize that if I want to have fun on vacation, it is up to me to do something to change a bad situation.

 Your Turn!

Now it is your turn to complete an essay (all the steps) like the one you just studied. Your assignment is to write an essay about the **different ideas/definitions of the perfect vacation.**

Step 1: Brainstorm and Questions

First start by asking yourself the questions from the beginning of this unit. Then try to brainstorm and write a list from the answers to your questions and brainstorming. Use the area below to record your words and phrases.

_____   _____   _____

_____   _____   _____

_____   _____   _____

_____   _____   _____

_____   _____   _____

Step 2: Outline

Choose the ideas and subtopics that relate to each other and that you are familiar enough with to write about. Then fill in the blanks of this outline format.

SUBJECT: Different Definitions of the Perfect Vacation

SUBTOPIC: _____

    Detail 1: _____

    Detail 2: _____

Add more details if you can.

SUBTOPIC: _____

    Detail 1: _____

    Detail 2: _____

Add more details if you can.

SUBTOPIC: _____

    Detail 1: _____

    Detail 2: _____

(Optional; if you can think of one or more subtopics, you can add them here and expand your outline.)

How did you do? What details did you think of that related to the perfect vacation? What were your subtopics? How many subtopics did you have? Look at the example brainstorming list and essay below. The essay is about different definitions of the perfect vacation. Does it have ideas similar to the ones in your outline above?

Example Brainstorm and List

beach	read books	spa
work in garden	hotel	free time
no work at office	new places	overseas
mountains	sightseeing	fun classes
exciting	day camp	mountain climbing
surfing	sleep late	no school
do nothing	cruise	relax
volunteer	no housework	different
Internet chat	eat good food	television
ideal	camping	meet others

EXAMPLE ESSAY

If you ask most students or workers for a definition of the word *vacation*, they usually say it is "time away from school or from work." If you ask them for a definition of *perfect*, their answer is probably something like "ideal, complete, the best possible." When they combine the two words to talk about a perfect vacation, their answers will be different, mostly depending on their moods when you ask for the definition.

When people are looking for stimulation on a perfect vacation, they could have two extremes in mind. If they like physical stimulation, they might enjoy the challenge of mountain climbing, white-water rafting, bicycling, or maybe attending a bodybuilding camp or a health spa. For a slightly easier workout, they might choose a walking tour. If they want intellectual stimulation on their perfect vacation, visiting museums is always popular. They can also choose short-term classes where they may study a foreign language in another country or attend a science camp in the mountains or near an ocean.

The concept of "service" can be used to describe two more different kinds of perfect vacations. When people like to receive service, they might enjoy staying at a luxury hotel or going on an ocean cruise. They can enjoy delicious meals without the work of planning, grocery shopping, cooking, and most of all, without having to clean up afterwards. In fact, there is a service person who takes care of every chore, from cleaning their rooms to doing their laundry. If people feel in the mood to give rather than receive service, there are agencies that arrange for volunteers to go to different locations to serve others. Some of the possibilities are teaching, sometimes on an American Indian reservation or perhaps teaching English in a developing country. Volunteers also sometimes go on archeological digs to do physical labor for the experts, or sometimes they go to underdeveloped areas to assist in building houses, schools, or hospitals.

A still different kind of perfect vacation doesn't relate to stimulation or service; its goal is total freedom from the clock. If people with vacation time decide to get up at noon, or not to get up at all, no problem. Eating whatever, whenever or wherever they want is easy. For example, ice cream for breakfast in bed is not only possible, it's a great idea! Choosing what to wear or even whether to wear anything at all is a no-brainer, at least when these perfect vacations take place at home. Spending hour after hour playing video games, chatting on the Internet, watching non-stop television, or reading the kinds of books or magazines that they would never have to read for school or their job are all wonderful ways to spend vacation time. Many times, simply staring into space for hours can be very satisfying on a perfect vacation.

The definition of a perfect vacation obviously varies. The concept of "complete" and "ideal" can change depending on people's moods when it is actually time for a vacation. Most importantly, a perfect vacation takes people away from their sometimes rather boring routines, and it helps them feel relaxed and ready to return to their daily school or work life after their vacation time has ended.

EXTRA!

In general, a number of topics and issues are commonly assigned for academic essays in classes like History, Science, Social Studies, and English. For practice and further reference, a few are listed.

politics/government	the environment	international relations
economics	health/medicine	education
crime	the law	family problems
traditions/customs	food	fashion
architecture	technology	superstitions
transportation	art	the future
machines	science	history
animals	places to live	sports
careers	the media	marriage
male/female roles	dating	movies
music	books	magazines
the Internet	television	pets

If you do not receive a specific writing assignment and are on your own to decide what to write about, think about issues that cause you to have strong feelings or a topic about which you know a lot, and write about one of them.

An Essay Plan from Topic to Final Draft

3.1 The Essay

Below is a standard essay format used at the writer's discretion. It is provided here as a springboard for beginning writers. The type of essay, in many cases, may require fewer or more body paragraphs as can be seen in the sample essays in Units 4 and 6. For example, the Sample Comparison Essay in Unit 4 has two body paragraphs, the Sample Process Essay in Unit 4 has four body paragraphs, and the revised Student Narrative Essay in Unit 6 has five body paragraphs.

INTRODUCTORY PARAGRAPH
1. General statements
2. Thesis statement

BODY PARAGRAPH 1
1. Topic sentence = Reason #1 for Thesis Statement
2. Supporting detail or example
3. Supporting detail or example
4. Supporting detail or example

BODY PARAGRAPH 2
1. Topic sentence = Reason #2 for Thesis Statement
2. Supporting detail or example

  3. Supporting detail or example
  4. Supporting detail or example

BODY PARAGRAPH 3

  1. Topic sentence = Reason #3 for Thesis Statement
  2. Supporting detail or example
  3. Supporting detail or example
  4. Supporting detail or example

CONCLUDING PARAGRAPH

  1. Restatement of the thesis statement
  2. Final comment on overall topic <u>or</u> summary of main points in the essay

DETAIL VERSUS EXAMPLE

A strong body paragraph uses details and examples to support the paragraph's topic sentence. What is the difference between an example and a detail? An **example** is a **concrete illustration that proves your topic sentence to be true**. A **detail** is a **specific piece of information that helps the reader understand more about the example**.

Topic Sentence:	The country's leader is not performing well.
Example:	The national unemployment rate has risen consistently since he was elected.
Detail #1:	Many manual laborers have lost their jobs this year because of cheaper labor in other countries.
Detail #2:	More people have filed for unemployment insurance this year than at anytime in the past 10 years.
Detail #3:	Some unemployed people have given up actively looking for jobs because they are discouraged by the complete lack of available work.

In your body paragraph, you can use one example with some details about that example, or you can choose to use a few examples which are not detailed. It is your choice as the writer.

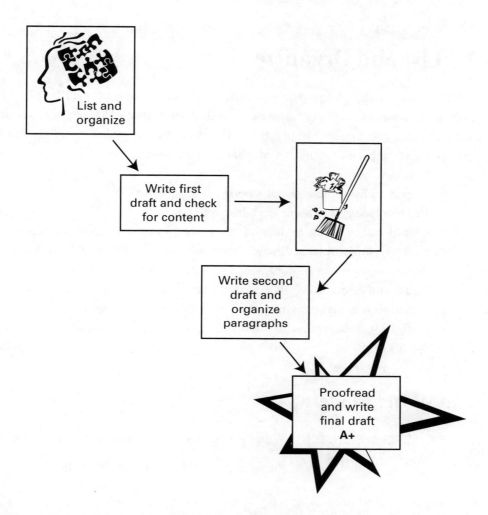

This section will take you through each step of the writing process with one model assignment called the Write! Model. The process has been divided into four basic steps:

1. listing and organizing ideas
2. writing the first draft and checking it for content
3. writing the second draft and checking for organization
4. proofreading for mechanics and writing the final draft

Each step will be described in detail and then modeled through a sample essay. Be sure to read each explanation and then examine how it has been applied in the Write! Model. This section will give you the knowledge and confidence you need to actually write essays in Unit 4. Are you ready? Let's begin!

3.2 List and Organize

You have been assigned to write an essay. Most likely, the essay will be one of seven main types of English essays. Unit 4 will discuss each of the essay types in detail and give you a chance to practice each one, but for now, here is a list of the essay types and a brief explanation of what each one does.

1. **Narrative Essay:** tells about a personal experience
2. **Process Essay:** teaches or explains a process
3. **Classification Essay:** divides a basic topic into three or more subtopics
4. **Comparison/Contrast Essay:** shows similarities and/or differences between two or more subtopics
5. **Cause and Effect Essay:** shows actions and results related to a specific topic
6. **Persuasion Essay:** convinces the reader of some aspect of the topic
7. **Definition Essay:** explains what the topic means to the reader and/or to other groups

The Write! Model

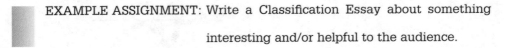

EXAMPLE ASSIGNMENT: Write a Classification Essay about something interesting and/or helpful to the audience.

Knowing what kind of essay to write is helpful, but what topic are you going to choose for the essay? This is something you often have to decide on your own. In order to decide on a topic that fits your essay type and also your audience, you need to **THINK** before you even begin composing. How much do you actually know about different topics? What aspects of a topic will you write about? In order to write successfully, you must sort out your ideas and ask yourself questions. This is called **LISTING AND ORGANIZING IDEAS.** There are two methods. Use both of them in the order they are presented.

Method 1: Self-Interview

With this method, you ask yourself a number of questions in order to come up with lots of different topics. You did a similar exercise in Unit 2. Additional questions will help you understand what you know and think about the topic and then assist you in narrowing your topic. You can use these same questions with any type of essay.

Questions for Self-Interview
1. What topics does this type of essay make me think of?
2. With which of these topics do I have personal experience or knowledge? What are those personal experiences and/or knowledge?
3. How can I interest readers in these topics? Are some of the topics more interesting than the others?
4. How can I show my opinions and/or feelings about these topics? About which topic do I have the strongest feelings?
5. About which one topic do I have the most to say? (Look at answers to Questions 3 and 4 and decide.)
6. What are some words or phrases that I think about in connection with this topic?
7. Ask yourself these questions, and record all your answers in sentences, words, or phrases. Remember that you will not use everything you write down, but write it down anyway so that you have many ideas to choose from. See the Write! Model example.

EXAMPLE 1: Self-Interview for Classification Essay
Question 1: What topics does this type of essay make me think of?
- ways to date
- ways to meet people
- types of popular cars
- kinds of houses

Question 2: With which of these topics do I have personal experience or knowledge? What are those personal experiences and/or knowledge?
- blind dates
- have had good and bad blind date experiences
- have met people in strange and unusual ways
- singles bars
- don't know anything about cars
- houseboats
- condos
- apartments

Question 3: How can I interest readers in these topics? Are some of the topics more interesting than the others?

- tell funny dating stories
- give advice on ways to meet people that would be relevant to men and women
- explain people's choices of house according to cost and size (boring?)

Question 4: How can I show my opinions and/or feelings about these topics? About which topic do I have the strongest feelings?

- strong feelings about dating because it is something that I do and my friends do
- lots of people do
- there are effective ways to date and meet people
- effects on people's lives (men and women)
- no real strong opinions about housing—just facts

Question 5: About which one topic do I have the most to say? (Look at answers to Questions 3 and 4 and decide.)

- dating
- how to meet people for dating
- had more information about this than about housing and kinds of housing

Question 6: What are some words or phrases that I think about in connection with this topic?

- blind date
- no more singles bars
- safety
- fun
- pressures
- nervousness

Method 2: Thought Webs

Now that you have narrowed your topic, it is time to start generating specific details and examples that you can use in your writing. To do this, you can visually organize your ideas as you think of them. Start by drawing a large circle in the middle of your paper. In the circle, write your main topic. Then record any thought, words, or phrases in smaller circles outside the larger one. Connect these smaller circles to form a picture like a web. Look at the example on page 35.

Write! Model

EXAMPLE 2: Thought Web for Classification Essay

TOPIC: Dating

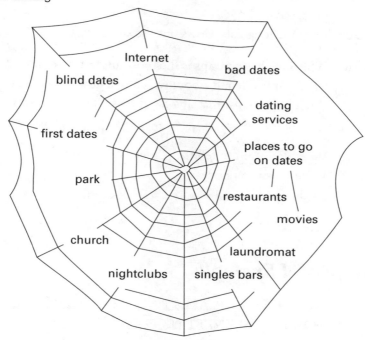

Internet

bad dates

blind dates

dating services

first dates

places to go on dates

park

restaurants

movies

church

laundromat

nightclubs   singles bars

Great! You now have a picture of specific ideas and possible details for your essay. It is time to decide which of them you will use and which you will cross out. You have to eliminate. Think about the type of essay you have been assigned. It is not possible to use all your ideas because your essay would go in too many directions.

In order to narrow your final topic, look at the clusters of ideas in your web and ask yourself the following questions:

ASK: Do all the items in my web relate to each other?
DO: Keep the ones that are related and cross out the other ones.

ASK: How many different groups can I make with all these phrases/words?
DO: Keep the long lists. Cross out the short ones.

ASK: Which of these groups is the most interesting to me? Which has the most detail? About which one do I feel the strongest?
DO: Circle the one list that answered these three questions. Cross out the rest.

ASK: What do I want to tell the readers about this topic?
DO: Write down some ideas.

Write! Model Example

TYPES OF DATES	PLACES TO MEET PEOPLE	PLACES TO DATE
first dates	park	restaurants
bad dates	singles bars	movies
blind dates	church	
	laundromat	
	Internet	
	nightclubs	

The heading Places to Meet People has the most topics, so you will be able to develop the strongest essay with this topic. The next step is to take this list and build an **OUTLINE.** An **OUTLINE** will help you organize your ideas, and it will be used as the plan for the essay. Look at the Write! Model Outline on page 37.

ASSIGNMENT: Classification essay to interest and teach the audience

Subject: Ways to meet a dating partner

1. General idea: It is becoming more difficult to find a date.

    Thesis statement: People are inventing creative new ways to meet each other.

2. Subtopic 1: laundromat

    Subtopic 2: walking the dog at the park

    Subtopic 3: Internet

WOW! See how much time has been spent just on listing and organizing your ideas? You will be happy to know that half of your writing job is FINISHED!

3.3 Write First Draft and Check for Content

Every essay has a purpose and a message. The type of essay you are assigned to write will help you choose your topic and narrow down the kinds of information (details, examples, stories) that you use, but then you need to **tell** the reader what you are going to discuss in your essay. This must be done early in the essay, so that the reader knows what will happen in the essay, and this will actually be a kind of map to guide you through the essay. This can be done in one sentence called the **THESIS STATEMENT.**

THESIS STATEMENT

You should remember from Unit 1 that this one sentence at the beginning of your essay tells the reader what to expect and shows the reader where you (the writer) will go with the essay. It shows the direction and announces what will be shown or taught in the essay. The **THESIS STATEMENT** must be specific and clear. There is only <u>one</u> thesis statement in an essay because you should have only <u>one</u> job to do in an essay. Once the thesis statement is written, the rest of the essay is easy to do. For this reason, the thesis statement should be the first sentence you write for your essay.

Your thesis statement is a promise to your reader that you are going to talk about a particular aspect of your topic. You must keep this promise by giving details, examples, and/or stories. This information will prove that your thesis statement is true.

BODY PARAGRAPHS

The details, examples, facts, and/or stories that prove that the thesis statement is true are written in the **BODY PARAGRAPHS** of the essay. Just like humans, an essay cannot exist without a strong body. These paragraphs help the reader understand your message. Each body paragraph is related to the thesis statement, but each one discusses a different part of the main topic. For this reason, each body paragraph must have its own topic sentence as you reviewed in Unit 1.

 # Your Turn!

Look at the following rough draft for the ongoing Write! Model. After you read it, circle the thesis statement. Put a box around the topic sentence in each body paragraph. (A complete introductory paragraph has not been deveoped yet.)

thesis

Innovative methods aimed at finding a dating partner are being successfully used by many singles today.

T.S

One new place at which singles can meet is the laundromat. There are two main ways you can strike up a conversation with a member of the opposite sex. The first way is by purposely dropping pieces of clothing as you move your laundry from one place to another and pass by your prospective interest on the way. In this case, the target will most likely pick up the clothing and return it to you. At this time, you can begin a conversation or buy your new interest a cup of coffee to show your gratitude. Another laundromat tactic plays on ignorance. You can act as if you have never been in a laundromat before and need some help. A woman may well act impressed at a man's attempts to sort, wash, and fold. Along these same lines, you could deliberately make a laundry mistake like mixing darks and lights. A deliberate cry for help attracts attention. If the laundromat is not for you, there is another location which may suit you better.

T.S

Dog owners are growing in numbers and it may have something to do with the great help dogs can give you when looking for a date. Taking your dog, preferably a puppy, on a leisurely walk in the park is an ideal way to attract attention. This "pick-up" method is more effective with male dog-walkers and female passers-by, but can work for both men and women. Pick your location well, and stroll by with your dog. Verbally communicating gently with the dog and frequently reaching down to pet or scratch the dog are clear signs of compassion and warmth. These are attractive qualities that men and women look for in a partner. If you "accidentally" let the leash extend far enough so that your dog licks or rubs against your prospective date, you will have the opportunity to begin a conversation. Often times, just walking your cute dog (no pitbulls or doberman pinschers) will attract people wanting to talk to and touch your dog. Finally, the surest way to use your dog to make a love connection is by mingling with other dog owners. Dog parks, dog beaches, doggy daycare centers, kennel clubs, and dog playgroups are guaranteed to have their share of love-hungry singles disguised as dog lovers. Maybe you don't have a dog or can't even borrow one for the day. There is a more private way to meet people without ever leaving home.

T.S

The most popular new way for singles to meet each other today is through the Internet. Now, in the comfort of your home office or bedroom, you can "talk" with singles anywhere in the world. In chat rooms or through classified ads posted on website bulletin boards, you can advertise any way you wish. Specialized chat rooms dedicated to certain religious affiliations, sports, music, hobbies, schools, or occupations allow you to weed out the individuals you have no interest in dating. This new kind of communication, whether written or oral with the help of computer microphones, can be done without worrying about what to wear or how to fix your hair. After meeting someone via the Internet, you may continue to date for some time in the same way before you eventually meet face to face. Of course, with this kind of anonymous dating, there is the risk of false representation regarding appearance, wealth, marital status and occupation. However, secure sites and ones that require photographs claim to be safe dating havens for many singles.

(A concluding paragraph has not been added yet.)

CONTENT

After you write the rough draft of your essay, it is necessary that you have a clear thesis statement and that every body paragraph has a topic sentence. The thesis statement for this essay is: **Many singles are successfully using innovative methods aimed at finding a dating partner today.** There are three topic sentences because there are three body paragraphs. The three topic sentences are:

1. One new place at which singles can meet is the laundromat.
2. Dog owners are growing in numbers and it may have something to do with the great help dogs can give you when looking for a date.
3. The most popular new way for singles to meet each other today is through the Internet.

Other questions that you should ask yourself about your first draft include questions about unity and clarity.

ASK: Does the information in each body paragraph relate directly to the topic sentence of that particular body paragraph?

ASK: Does each body paragraph cover only ONE aspect of the main topic?

ASK: Have I tried to show rather than tell? (See page 80.)

ASK: Have I accidentally written the same thing in more than one paragraph?

ASK: Is my thesis statement clear and accurate? Do I really discuss parts of my thesis statement in each of the body paragraphs?

3.4 Write Second Draft

You have written your first draft and checked it for content. Now it is important to provide a full introduction to your thesis statement and a conclusion to your essay. Readers need to have some background information about the subject in order to understand your ideas about it. If readers do not have this information, it is hard for them to completely understand and appreciate the body of your essay. Remember from Unit 1 that the introduction comes directly before the thesis statement; it is a way to lead into your thesis statement. This paragraph is called the **INTRODUCTORY PARAGRAPH,** and the last sentence of this paragraph is your thesis statement.

INTRODUCTORY PARAGRAPH

The INTRODUCTORY PARAGRAPH is the first paragraph of your essay that the audience reads. Therefore, this paragraph has the important job of

- attracting the attention of the reader
- introducing the main idea with general ideas, opinions, and/or facts
- presenting your thesis statement

This paragraph can start with general statements or an anecdote about your topic and then narrow in order to help lead into your thesis statement. It must be interesting and clear. If readers are bored or confused by your introductory paragraph, they will not want to read the rest of your essay.

Look at the example paragraph from the Write! Model.

> "It's so hard to meet people." "All the good ones are either gay or married." These days, people are finding it more and more difficult to form dating relationships. Singles bars are saturated with desperate people looking for Mr. or Miss Right. The practice of blind dating has virtually disappeared. As a result, singles today are being forced to create new ways to meet each other. Some innovative methods aimed at finding a dating partner are being successfully used by many singles.

(Notice how the other sentences in the introductory paragraph lead into the thesis statement that has already been written.)

CONCLUDING PARAGRAPH

The last paragraph of an essay, you'll recall, is the **CONCLUDING PARAGRAPH.** This paragraph eases readers out of the essay and urges them to think further about the subject. Without this paragraph, readers would feel as if the essay ended suddenly and that perhaps the writer had not finished the essay. The job of the concluding paragraph is to summarize the essay; sometimes writers restate (use different words for) their thesis statements in the concluding paragraph. This paragraph also may (but not always) leave the reader with a fresh idea or question regarding the overall message of the essay.

Look at an example concluding paragraph from the Write! Model.

> Whether it be in a dog park, a laundromat, or in front of their computer, today's singles are creating unusual means to find suitable dating partners. They are avoiding traditional methods of singles bars and blind dates and creating a new trend in the search for that special someone.

> These new practices show that singles are ready to mingle. Undreamed of ten years ago, these new practices have and probably will continue to evolve into even more imaginative methods of finding dating partners.

(Notice how the last sentence conveys the same idea as the thesis statement.)

It is time to look at the second draft of the Write! Model essay with some changes in the body paragraphs and the addition of the introductory and concluding paragraphs. What kinds of changes do you notice? How is the revised essay better than the first draft?

Write! Model Second Draft: Classification Essay on Ways to Meet People to Date

"It's so hard to meet people." "All the good ones are either gay or married." These days, people are finding it more and more difficult to form dating relationships. Singles bars are saturated with desperate people looking for Mr. or Miss Right. The practice of blind dating has virtually disappeared. As a result, singles today are being forced to create new ways to meet each other. Some innovative methods aimed at finding a dating partner are being successfully used by many singles.

One new place where singles can meet is the laundromat. There are two main ways you can strike up a conversation with a man or woman. First, you can purposely drop pieces of clothing while you move your laundry from one place to another. Be careful to drop the piece as you walk in front of the person who interests you. In this case, the target of your interest will most likely pick up the clothing and return it to you. At this time, you can begin a conversation or buy your new interest a cup of coffee to show your gratitude. Another laundromat tactic plays on ignorance. You can act as if you have never been in a laundromat before and need some help. A woman may well act impressed at a man's attempts to sort, wash, and fold. Along these same lines, you could deliberately make a laundry mistake like mixing darks and lights. These deliberate cries for help attract attention. If the laundromat is not for you, there is another location which may suit you better.

Dog owners are growing in numbers and this fact may be related to the help dogs give you when looking for a date. Taking your dog, preferably a puppy, on a leisurely walk is an ideal way to attract attention. This "pick-up" method is more effective with male dog-walkers and female passers-by, but can work for both men and women. Pick your location well, and stroll by with your dog. Verbally communicating gently and frequently reaching down to pet or scratch the dog are clear signs of your compassion and warmth. These are attractive qualities that both men and women look for in a partner. If you "accidentally" let the leash extend far enough so that your dog licks or rubs against the prospective date, you will have the opportunity to begin a conversation. Often times, just walking your cute dog (no pit bulls or doberman pinschers) will attract people who want to talk to and touch your dog. Finally, the surest way to use your dog to make a love connection is by mingling with other dog owners. Dog parks, dog beaches, doggy daycare centers, kennel clubs, and dog play-groups are guaranteed to provide their share of love-hungry singles who are disguised as dog lovers. Maybe you don't have a dog or can't even borrow one for the day. In this case, there is a more private way to meet people from your home.

Now, in the comfort of your home office or bedroom, you can "talk" with singles anywhere in the world. In chat rooms or through classified ads posted on website bulletin boards, you can advertise any way you wish. Specialized chat rooms dedicated to certain religious affiliations, sports, music, hobbies, schools, or occupations allow you to weed out the individuals you have no interest in dating. This new kind of communication, either written or oral with the help of computer microphones, can be done without worrying about what to wear or how to fix your hair. After meeting someone via the Internet, you may continue to "date" for some time in the same way before you eventually meet face to face. Of course, with this kind of anonymous dating, there is the risk of false representation regarding appearance, wealth, marital status, and occupation. However, secure sites and ones that require photographs claim to be safe dating havens for many singles.

Whether it be in a dog park, a laundromat, or in front of their computer, today's singles are creating unusual means to find suitable dating partners. They are avoiding traditional methods of singles bars and blind dates, and creating a new trend in the search for that special someone. These new practices show that singles are ready to mingle. Undreamed of ten years ago, these new practices have and probably will continue to evolve into even more imaginative methods of finding dating partners.

Got It!
The Parts of an Essay

Let's stop for a review of the essay format. Refer to the diagram on page 28 if you need help. How many questions can you answer correctly without looking at the diagram?

QUESTION 1:   Which paragraph introduces the main idea for the whole essay? Where is it in the essay?

ANSWER: The _____ paragraph is the first/ second/third/fourth/fifth paragraph of the essay.

QUESTION 2:   The final sentence in the first paragraph states the main idea of the whole essay. What is it called?

ANSWER: That sentence is called the _____.

QUESTION 3:   How many paragraphs are in an average essay excluding the first and last paragraphs?

ANSWER: The body of the essay usually has _____ paragraphs.

QUESTION 4:   In the body of the essay, the first sentence in each body paragraph introduces the topic for that paragraph.

ANSWER: That sentence is called the

_____.

QUESTION 5:   Which paragraph summarizes what has been said and concludes the essay?

ANSWER: The _____ paragraph is the first/second/third/final paragraph of the essay.

3.5 Proofread and Write Final Draft

How did you do on the review? Were you able to identify the parts of an essay and what they do? If you have been looking at the formation of the Write! Model carefully, your answers were probably all correct. Finally, you are at the last step of the writing process. This is the point at which you polish your essay; you make sure the punctuation, capitalization, spelling, individual word choice, and grammar are correct. All of these elements are called the **MECHANICS** of the essay. In Unit 5, you can do exercises that will help you learn about specific areas of mechanics and how to recognize and fix problems.

There is actually a checklist you can use when proofreading your essay. The checklist is a list of questions that you can ask yourself about your essay as you go over it line by line. In Unit 4, you will be given seven different checklists, each one to fit one specific essay type. For now, however, let's look at a simple mechanics checklist. The answers to all of these questions should, of course, be **YES!**

Mechanics Checklist

YES	NO	
_____	_____	Does each sentence have a subject, a verb, and a complete thought?
_____	_____	Does each sentence begin with a capital letter and end with a period?
_____	_____	Do all the word combinations (subject-verb, adjective-noun, noun-pronoun) agree with each other?
_____	_____	Does the verb tense express the appropriate time in each sentence?
_____	_____	Are all the words spelled correctly?
_____	_____	Are the articles *(a, an, the)* used correctly?
_____	_____	Are the forms of the words (verb, noun, adjective) used correctly?
_____	_____	Are all the word choices appropriate?
_____	_____	Are all the sentences in correct order?

Got It!
Proofreading

You will notice that the second draft of the Write! Model essay does not have any mechanical problems because we did not want to confuse you as you read the essay. However, in order for you to understand what is meant by **PROOFREADING**, below is one part of the Write! Model essay. This part has 14 mechanical errors. See if you can find the errors and then correct them. An explanation of each mechanical error follows, but do not peek!!!

1 Dog owners. Growing in numbers and it may have something to do

2 with the great help dogs can give you when looking for date. Taking

3 your dog, preferably a puppy, on a leisurely walk is an ideal way to

4 attract attention. This "pick-up" method are more effective with male

5 dog-walkers and female passers-by, but can work for both men and

6 women. Picked your location well, and stroll by with your dog.

7 Verbally communicating gently and frequently reachng down to pet

8 or scratch dog are clear signs of your compassion and warmth. These

9 are attractive qualities that both men and women look for in a

10 partner. IF you "accidentally" let the leash extend far enough, so, that

11 your dog is licked or rubbed against the prospective date, you will

12 have the opportunity to begin a conversation Often times, just waling

13 your cute dog (no pitbulls or doberman pinschers) will attract people

14 who wish to talk to and touch your dog. Finally, the surest way to use

15 your dog to make a love connection is by mingling with other dog

16 owners at places like dog parks, dog beaches, doggy daycare centers,

17 kennel clubs, and dog playgroups that are guaranteed to have their

18 share of love-hungry singles who are disguised as dog lovers, but

19   maybe you don't have a dog nor can't even borrow one for the day.

20   There is a more private ways to meet people at home.

THE 14 MECHANICAL ERRORS: ANSWERS

Did you find all 14 errors? Look at the explanation below and then refer to the second draft of the Write! Model essay to see the mechanically correct last draft of the essay.

Error 1:   In line 1, **Dog owners** is a sentence fragment because it doesn't have a verb. It is not a complete sentence.

Error 2:   In lines 1 and 2, **Growing in numbers and it may have something to do with the great help dogs can give you when looking for date** is not a complete sentence. It is a sentence fragment like Error 1.

Error 3:   In line 2, **when looking for date** is missing an article in front of the noun *date*.

Error 4:   In line 4, the verb of this sentence is **are** and does not agree with the subject **method**.

Error 5:   In line 6, the first verb in this sentence **picked** does not match the form of the other verb in the sentence **stroll**. One verb is in the past tense and the other is in a command form. The sentence is in the form of a command, and therefore the form of the first verb should be changed.

Error 6:   In line 8, **scratch dog** is missing an article in front of the noun **dog**.

Error 7:   In line 10, **IF** should not be in all capital letters.

Error 8:   In line 10, **so** does not need commas on either side of it; **so that** is sufficient and no commas are necessary.

Error 9:   In line 11, the verbs *is licked* and **rubbed** have been written in passive voice, but they need to be written in active voice. In that sentence, those two verbs describe what the dog does, not what is done to the dog.

Error 10:   In line 12, there is no period after the last word in the sentence (**conversation**).

Error 11:   In line 12, **waling** should be **walking**. This is a spelling error.

Error 12:   In lines 14–19, ***Finally, the surest way to use your dog to make a love connection is by mingling with other dog-owners at places like dog parks, dog beaches, doggy daycare centers, kennel clubs, and dog playgroups that are guaranteed to have their share of love-hungry singles who are disguised as dog-lovers, but maybe you don't have a dog nor can't even borrow one for the day.*** is a run-on sentence. The sentence is too long; there is too much information in one sentence. This part of the paragraph should be divided into three separate sentences.

Error 13:   In line 19, ***don't have a dog nor can't even . . .*** has two negatives in the phrase. One of the negatives needs to be changed to a positive.

Error 14:   In line 20, the singular article at the beginning of ***a more private ways*** and the plural noun (***ways***) do not agree.

If you aren't sure you understand all of these types of mistakes, see your grammar textbook or ask your teacher.

Congratulations! You have just learned all the steps to writing a successful essay. Now it is time to learn about the different kinds of essays and what they do.

Examining Seven Types of Essays

4.1 The Narrative Essay

WHAT DOES IT DO?

- A **narrative essay** tells a story about a meaningful experience in the writer's life.
- It describes events related to that experience.
- It shows the reader the dominant impression the writer has of this experience.

WHAT DOES IT CONTAIN?

- A **narrative essay** has an introductory paragraph that states the experience and then leads to a thesis statement that identifies the writer's feelings about the experience.
- It has body paragraphs with specific examples that show how the experience caused the writer to have that feeling.
- It has a concluding paragraph that restates the thesis and summarizes the experience.

WHAT DOES IT DISCUSS?

Narrative essays are usually about the writer's life. Examples include childhood experiences, life-changing experiences, strange experiences, and once-in-a-lifetime experiences. This kind of essay is usually written in the past tense.

• SAMPLE NARRATIVE ESSAY •

A Memorable Wedding

Weddings are supposed to be joyous, memorable occasions. Most people show their wedding pictures to friends and family for years to come. I wish my wedding day had left such fond memories. My wedding day was a nightmare. From the planning to the day of the ceremony, everything that could possibly go wrong, did.

The uneasy beginning should have given me a hint that something bad was going to happen. My fiancé, Chul Soo, and I had decided to marry after having known each other for only three months. After many arguments with my parents about the issue, I left my parents' house and moved in with my future husband. As soon as we started living together, all our relatives began urging us to get married. We decided on a small ceremony, set the date, made homemade invitations, and I bought a simple white dress. I thought things were improving, but not for long.

The weekend of our wedding, my future father-in-law came from Korea, and his stay was very difficult for us. My future mother-in-law was so ill she couldn't come, and soon we learned that Chul Soo's brother's flight had been cancelled due to snow. Despite the fact that we were not yet married, Chul Soo's father stayed at our house, and he expected me to serve him in every way. I foolishly did what he expected: ironing his clothes, preparing huge meals, and driving him from place to place. I completely ignored the fact that I needed to prepare for my wedding. The "night before" came and I did not have shoes to wear to my own wedding. At 8:30 p.m., my future father-in-law and I hurried to the nearest shoe store where I finally found a decent pair of high-heels. It was a stormy February night and we had been together all day.

Then it was off to the grocery store to pick up the cake. That added more stress. We picked up the cake and saw blonde bride and groom plastic figurines on the top. These blondes did not resemble my Korean fiancé or my Italian self. We took the cake to the restaurant where the reception was to be held the next day following the wedding. As I took it out of the car, the cake fell against the side of its box. Consequently, I had two blonde figurines standing on a dented wedding cake. The owner of the restaurant and I set the cake strategically on a table in the corner. The dented side was against a wall. Then I got out a marker and started coloring the figurines' heads. As luck would have it, the marker ran out of ink. The bride had a full head of new black hair and the groom had a head of two colors. I was tired. Tomorrow was my wedding day. Those figurines would provide entertainment, I decided, mistakenly thinking tomorrow would be a better day.

My wedding morning was rushed and full of surprises. After the groom and groom's father had taken their morning showers,

I jumped in. There was NO SHAMPOO!! I had only an hour and a half before the wedding, so I actually washed my hair with body soap. That was a bad decision. Not too long after that, my hair started to expand sideways. It was out of control. I knew I couldn't deal with it, so I pulled all my hair back into a ponytail. Now what else could possibly go wrong?

I put the new jewelry set that Chul Soo's father had given me in the car, put my wedding dress in a dress bag and headed for the church. There, the minister informed us that he would not accept the vows we had written. He threw out our personally written vows and omitted the hymn *When East Meets West* which we had chosen to add a little religious humor to the occasion. I told myself, "Chin up!" and went into the bathroom to get ready. As I finished my make-up, I reached for the pretty red garnet necklace and matching earrings my future in-laws had given me. I must have been nervous because plop, plop, plop, the whole set dropped into the church toilet. I pulled them out, shook them off, and put them on. No one would know.

Now it was time to put on the wedding dress. I opened the dress bag to find my wedding dress in a pile at the bottom of the bag. I grabbed my best friend, and we drove as fast as we could to my apartment to iron the dress. At the front door, I realized I had no key. The parents of my best friend lived nearby, so we hurried there. "This could only happen to you, Jackie!" the best friend's mother repeated over and over as she laughed at me. I knew there was a reason I hadn't invited her to the wedding.

We rushed back to the church. I was traveling 88 miles per

hour in a 35 mile-per-hour zone. Soon we heard a siren and I saw a flashing red light in my rearview mirror. I did not have my driver's license with me. The policeman would not accept my explanation, and he escorted us to the church so I could get my license for him. By this time, I was late to my own wedding. The siren and flashing light in front of the church brought out all the guests. Only my fiancé looked happy; he thought I had changed my mind about marrying him. We were able to start the wedding as soon as the police car left.

We all calmed down and finally the ceremony commenced. After a wedding completely different from the one we had designed, we were officially declared husband and wife. Too much had happened that day! I'm glad we didn't go on a honeymoon!

EXAMINING THE NARRATIVE ESSAY

A **narrative essay** tells a story about a meaningful experience in the writer's life. The effect of the experience on the writer is identified as the dominant impression and is expressed in the thesis statement of the essay. The events that lead to the dominant impression are shown in the form of concrete examples in the body paragraphs of the essay.

In this sample essay the writer tells us in her thesis statement, "From the planning to the day of the ceremony, everything that could possibly go wrong, did." From this dominant impression of "a nightmare" before and during her wedding, the writer shows us, by the use of specific examples, how her experience led to her impression.

Your Turn!

Answer the following questions about *A Memorable Wedding* in order to understand the **narrative essay** and how it is constructed.

1. The first unpleasant event was the arrival of her future father-in-law. The writer shows us examples of herself serving him. What were those examples?
2. The next event involved the wedding cake. What was wrong with the cake?
3. The following event concerned her hair. What was the problem?
4. The next paragraph shows her troubles with the minister and her jewelry. Explain each problem.
5. Next came a problem with her house key. Explain.
6. Finally, an encounter with the police took place. What happened?

WRITE!

When you choose your topic for a **narrative essay,** it is essential that you select one of your experiences that can be broken into parts (specific examples) that will lead to and reinforce your dominant impression of the events (thesis statement).

Look at another **narrative essay** on page 147! Then try writing one yourself!

If you're having trouble thinking of a topic, here are some ideas for a **narrative essay.**

- a day I would like to relive
- an embarrassing experience
- a frightening event
- a disappointing happening
- an event that changed my life
- a surprising day

Checklist for a Narrative Essay

CONTENT

GOOD OK NEEDS WORK

____ ____ ____   The essay clearly expresses the writer's feelings about an event.

____ ____ ____   The essay includes the time and place of this event.

____ ____ ____   The essay makes clear which other people played a part in this event.

____ ____ ____   The essay uses "word pictures" to show the event.

ORGANIZATION

GOOD OK NEEDS WORK

____ ____ ____   The introductory paragraph leads to a thesis statement.

____ ____ ____   The thesis statement declares the event and the writer's feeling.

____ ____ ____   Each paragraph in the body has a topic sentence.

____ ____ ____   The body paragraphs follow a chronological order.

____ ____ ____   The body paragraphs connect to each other with transition words or phrases.

____ ____ ____   The essay builds to a high point or climax.

____ ____ ____   The concluding paragraph restates the thesis and summarizes the narrative.

MECHANICS

YES   NO

____   ____   Does each sentence have a subject, a verb, and a complete thought?

____   ____   Does each sentence begin with a capital letter and end with a period?

____   ____   Do all the word combinations (subject-verb, adjective-noun, noun-pronoun) agree with each other?

____   ____   Does the verb tense express the appropriate time in each sentence?

____   ____   Are all the words spelled correctly?

____   ____   Are the articles (a, an, the) used correctly?

____   ____   Are the forms of the words (verb, noun, adjective) used correctly?

____   ____   Are all the word choices appropriate?

____   ____   Are all the sentences in correct order?

Got It! Introductory and Concluding Paragraphs

Sometimes the hardest part of writing an essay is in creating its beginning, or **introductory paragraph**. It is a good idea to write at least some sort of beginning paragraph just to get your essay started. You can always go back to rewrite the introductory paragraph when you write later drafts of your essay.

You will find that writing the **concluding paragraph** is also much easier once you decide which introductory paragraph is your best one.

To show you how introductory and concluding paragraphs can be improved, we have removed them from another narrative essay. The following paragraphs form only **the body** of the essay. Read these three paragraphs. Then you will choose the best introductory and concluding paragraphs when you do the exercises that follow these body paragraphs.

My foreign travel before that time had been limited to traveling with my family, so all my needs were planned and carried out by someone else. Therefore, I looked forward to what I thought would be an adventure. After an overnight train trip, we arrived in Lisbon and started to look for cheap accommodations to save money for more exciting things later. We chose one of the cheapest hotels from the list at the train station. After we walked six city blocks with two heavy suitcases each, we reached the door of the hotel and decided it would be satisfactory because we didn't want to walk any farther with our luggage. We signed on for two nights, and this was when we learned why the hotel was so inexpensive. Our rooms were on the fifth floor, and there wasn't any elevator! By the time we reached our rooms, we also learned that in addition to sharing a bathroom with everyone else on our floor, we had a room with a door lock that worked only some of the time.

The other guests on the fifth floor were very noisy, so we got up early and decided that this would be our last day in Lisbon, and that we would go to one of the oldest and most famous areas of the city. I was worried about leaving anything valuable in my room with a door that might not lock, so I left the hotel with my light-weight shoulder strap traveling bag/purse stuffed with travelers' checks, plane tickets, Portuguese cash, credit card, and of course, my passport, just in case. After a trolley ride to our destination, we climbed up the steep walk to Saint George's castle and looked down on the area called Alfama, a neighborhood that is famous for its narrow, winding streets and beautiful buildings first constructed 800 years ago. Of course we had to have a closer look at it.

We quickly reached an inviting walkway that looked like a tunnel with steps leading down to another street. Awestruck by my surroundings, gawking all around and gushing to Nika who was a few steps ahead of me about how wonderful it all was, I was an easy mark, almost flashing a sign, "I am a stupid tourist. Rob me, please." Within seconds, a young man suddenly appeared out of the darkness. My heart raced as I felt the jerk on my shoulder when he either cut or wrenched the bag strap free. I yelled to Nika and started back up the stairs in pursuit.

Nika was a faster runner than I was, but because of all the shadowy places, it was impossible to find the young man. I remember how embarrassed I was when I had to tell Nika that I had put everything important in that purse, and no, I hadn't made photocopies of anything. Fortunately, there was a police station nearby. When the friendly officer filled out my official theft report, he said he was very sorry, but that I wouldn't be able to replace my passport, tickets and travelers checks for two days because the robbery was on Sunday and the next day was May first, a holiday in just about every country of the world except the United States.

Nika was far kinder than I deserved. Most importantly, she did not point out my stupidity in carrying everything with me or not making copies of my documents. We had to change our travel plans and stay at the Lisbon hotel for three extra days because we had to wait until Tuesday, the day after the holiday to make not one, but two trips to the American Embassy. We had to return a second time because I hadn't brought photos for a new passport. Trips to the travelers' checks, credit card and airline offices ate up the time that we had planned to spend at Faro, a beach resort. We finally got there, but by then our friendship was beginning to show strain, and I think neither one of us was sorry to separate once we were back in Spain. Nika was undoubtedly glad to be rid of me, and I was feeling too much guilt to enjoy myself.

1. *We have intentionally mixed up the order of the writer's revisions, so you will need to read each choice carefully before you decide which is the best introductory paragraph for this essay.*

   a.   The four-week Spanish lessons in Salamanca, Spain, had gone well. During the class sessions, I had become friends with Nika, who was from Finland. Both Nika and I had return flight tickets to our own countries scheduled a week after our Spanish class ended in Salamanca, so we decided to travel together to Portugal and make Lisbon our first stop. It was there that I had a very upsetting experience that was caused by my own stupidity.

   b.   In Lisbon, Portugal I had a very upsetting experience that was caused by my own stupidity. I have always liked to travel because I like to see and do different things. Sometimes I like to go to resorts for skiing or swimming, and sometimes I like to go to cities that have a lot of exciting things to see and do. I have had many different travel experiences, some good and some not so good.

   c.   Travel can be a great teacher. For example, I learned in Lisbon, Portugal, that it is not a good idea to carry all your valuables when you go sightseeing. I took my plane tickets, Portuguese cash, credit card and even my passport with me, and they were stolen. To make things worse, I had not made photocopies of my travel documents before I left the United States.

Now go back and read the essay again with its new introductory paragraph. Then choose the best concluding paragraph from the choices below.

2. *Read all three choices and decide which is the best concluding paragraph for this essay.*

    a.   Two days later, I flew home. The plane was not full, so I could lie across three seats to sleep a little. I was lucky because usually all the seats in economy class are taken, and there is not even enough room to sit comfortably. There were two young women smoking cigarettes on a non-smoking flight, but the flight attendants didn't seem to notice them. Someday I would like to have enough money to fly first class so that I could have more room, better food and no smoke.

    b.   I know that my problem in Lisbon was caused because I hadn't made an intelligent plan. This experience is something I still don't really like to think about, but it certainly changed the way I prepare for travel. Now I make copies, keep records, and always wear a money belt under my clothes. One positive thought remains; today I still regret the experience, but it didn't change my impression of Lisbon. It is still one of the most beautiful and interesting places I have ever seen, and I am very happy that I went there.

    c.   I really had fun during the time in Spain and most of the time in Portugal. The trouble started when I decided to take all my important travel documents with me because I didn't think the hotel room was secure. While we were sightseeing a thief took my purse, and we had to go to the police station. We had to wait two days to get copies of everything. Then we went to Faro and finally back to the airport in Madrid. It was stupid of me not to make copies of my passport and plane tickets.

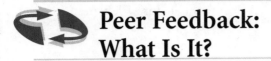

Peer Feedback:
What Is It?

Peer feedback is a way through which you, as a beginning writer, give feedback to fellow writers about their work and get feedback from those same peers. Reading and listening to what colleagues and classmates have to say about your writing helps you look at your writing through the audience's eyes. Sometimes the red ink and corrections from your teacher may leave you feeling discouraged and confused about your writing, not to mention that you may not agree with your teacher's corrections. When you receive feedback from fellow writers, you begin to see that some aspects of your writing—for example, serious grammatical errors or lack of transition between ideas—actually make other aspects of your writing difficult to understand, or maybe boring.

At the same time you are getting feedback, you are also giving it. You do so by reading and examining other classmates' writings. Sometimes you will be asked to look for specific problems; other times you will need to give general feedback about how much you understood an essay or how you felt after you read it. When you read another person's writing, although you automatically compare your own writing to your peer's, the real purpose is for you to discover new and better ways to structure a sentence or to sequence sentences in a paragraph. Maybe you'll encounter a new vocabulary word that you could use in your writing. You'll also observe errors in content and structure and, as a result, become more careful not to make those same mistakes in your own writing.

The Peer Feedback Form can be used the next time a teacher or a classmate asks you to read a peer's work and give feedback. This is a general form, but sometimes you'll be looking for specific points that your peer is hoping to focus on and strengthen. At the end of each of the following sections, there are three to five additional peer feedback questions. You can add some or all of those questions to this larger form. Or you can use the smaller lists to focus on a more specific area of writing. Most of the time, peer feedback is done anonymously, so you should not be afraid to be honest and specific when you tell your fellow writer what you think about his or her writing.

Peer Feedback Form

After you read your classmate's essay completely, answer the following questions. You may need to reread the essay in order to answer honestly and thoroughly. Remember that your peer is counting on you to give honest feedback. Be specific, and, most important, tell your peer what you really think.

(CIRCLE ONE)

1. **True   False**   I understood what the writer was trying to say.

2. **True   False**   There was a clear thesis statement in this essay.

   It was: _____

   _____

3. **True   False**   Each body paragraph had a clear topic sentence.

   The topic sentences were: _____

   _____

   _____

   _____

   _____

4. **True   False**   Grammatical mistakes made this writing difficult to under-

   stand. One mistake I noticed was: _____

   _____

   _____

   _____.

5.   For this question, you'll write two adjectives. Overall, this essay was

   _____, but also _____.

4.2 The Process Essay

WHAT DOES IT DO?

- A **process essay** shows how a task or a process is completed.
- It lists the steps or stages of the process in a logical, sequential order and explains each step or stage in detail.
- It teaches or retells the process.

WHAT DOES IT CONTAIN?

- A **process essay** begins with a paragraph that introduces the topic and then leads to a thesis statement that clearly states what process will be described in the essay.
- Each paragraph in the body describes one necessary step of the process and uses clear, concise directions.
- This essay has sequence signals. Sequence signals are words that indicate the order in which steps or events happen in an essay. The most commonly used sequence signals are *first, second, third,* etc., but to make the essay more interesting it is good to use a variety of sequence signals. Other sequence signals include *next, after that, simultaneously, before, then, at the same time.* Verbs can also indicate sequence, for example: *continue, start, begin,* and *follow.*
- This essay concludes with a restatement of the thesis and a summary of the process.

WHAT DOES IT DISCUSS?

A **process essay** can discuss a simple hands-on project like making a pizza, or it can discuss something more abstract like finding an apartment or choosing a pet. Whatever the topic, the essay discusses a process from beginning to end. The essay can be written in the past or future tense, but it is usually written in the present tense.

• SAMPLE PROCESS ESSAY •

Finding a Place to Live

Moving to a new town can be difficult and confusing. Everything is new. Maybe you do not know anyone. You cannot find your way around easily. You may not even speak the same language as the local people. You may be living with friends or at a hotel which can be depressing and only a short-term solution to your living situation. To make your life easier and more pleasant, you need to find a place to rent. This is a painless process which involves four simple steps.

Before you start to look for your new home, you need to make a list about the kind of home you would like to have. Begin by asking yourself questions. Do I want to live in a house or in an apartment? How many bedrooms do I need? How much rent can I afford each month? Will I need a place that takes pets? Do I want to pay extra for utilities? Use the answers to these questions to form a description of the place you want. Now you are ready to start looking.

The easiest place to look for places to rent is in the newspaper's classified section. The ads are organized in sections: houses for rent, apartments, and condominiums. If the city or area is large, the ads will be listed according to neighborhoods. You will find the same information in most ads: the number of bedrooms (1BR, 2BR, 3BR), the number of bathrooms (1BA, 2BA), the monthly rent, the required deposit, and whether utilities are included in the rent. Some ads tell you the address and whether or not utilities (electricity, water, trash) are included in the rent.

Some ads tell you the address and whether pets are allowed. The ad will always have a phone number and sometimes a name for you to contact if you are interested. Mark the places that fit your requirements and then call and make an appointment to see these places.

Always look at a prospective home with the owner or manager of the building. When you arrive at your appointment, it is important that you look at the place carefully and ask a few vital questions to help you make your decision. Look at the paint on the ceilings and walls. Is it new? Are there water stains or chipped paint? Take a look at the bathroom—the bathtub, shower, and toilet. Turn the water on. Is the hot water hot enough? Does the toilet flush properly? Does water drip onto the floor when you turn on the shower? Are the carpets stained? Do the windows all open and shut? Do the locks on the doors work? Ask the landlord or manager how old the place is, and who lived there previously. Ask what costs you would be responsible for. Could you paint or decorate if you wanted to do so? Would you have to pay in order to put nails in the walls? Spend a long time looking at two or three places. Compare them and then make your decision.

Once you have decided, you will need to sign a lease. The lease is an agreement between you and the owner. It is usually a one- or two-page document that lists all the rules both you and the owner have to follow. It will include information about the rent, the deposit, pets, utility payments, deposit for damages, and most importantly, the length of time that you can live in the place. Most are one-year leases, but there are also six-month leases.

Always read the lease completely before you sign it. After it is signed, you have a new home.

Renting an apartment or a house is a simple, four-step process. Decide what you want, look for it in the newspapers, set an appointment to see the place, inspect it carefully, and then sign a lease. In a few days, you should be able to find the home to fit your budget and your choice. A new home in a new city will help you begin to feel like you really belong.

EXAMING THE PROCESS ESSAY

A **process essay** shows or teaches how a task or process is completed. It explains each necessary step or phase of the process in sequential order.

The thesis of this essay states, "This [finding your own home] is a painless process which involves four steps." Following this thesis, the essay lists each of those steps and explains how to complete each one.

 # Your Turn!

Answer the following questions about *Finding a Place to Live* in order to understand the **process essay** and how it was constructed.

1. First, what kind of list should you make before you begin looking for your own home?
2. What is some of the information that you will find about houses or apartments in a newspaper's classified section?
3. What are some important questions that you should ask the person who shows you a house or an apartment?
4. What is the final step of this process?

WRITE!

When you choose a topic for your **process essay,** you need to think of a task, a project, or even a scientific phenomenon that you know about from actual experience. A topic that can be divided into three or four reasonably simple steps works well for a process essay.

Look at another **process essay** on page 151! Then try writing one yourself!

If you're having trouble thinking of a topic, here are some ideas for a **process essay.**

- how to play (a simple game)
- how to make _____
- how to buy a car
- how to do well in a class

- how to be a good babysitter (or other job)
- how to host a party

Checklist for a Process Essay

CONTENT

GOOD OK NEEDS WORK

____ ____ ____ The essay thoroughly explains how to follow a process.

____ ____ ____ The essay includes all the necessary steps to complete a process.

____ ____ ____ The essay clearly shows how to complete each step of a process.

____ ____ ____ The essay uses "word pictures" to show the process.

ORGANIZATION

GOOD OK NEEDS WORK

____ ____ ____ The introductory paragraph leads to a thesis statement.

____ ____ ____ The thesis statement clearly declares what process is to be explained.

____ ____ ____ Each paragraph in the body begins with a topic sentence.

____ ____ ____ The body paragraphs follow a logical order to show completion of the process.

____ ____ ____ The body paragraphs connect to each other with transition words or phrases.

____ ____ ____ The concluding paragraph restates the thesis and summarizes the process.

MECHANICS

YES NO

____ ____ Does each sentence have a subject, a verb, and a complete thought?

____ ____ Does each sentence begin with a capital letter and end with a period?

____ ____ Do all the word combinations (subject-verb, adjective-noun, noun-pronoun) agree with each other?

____ ____ Does the verb tense express the appropriate time in each sentence?

____ ____ Are all the words spelled correctly?

____ ____ Are the articles (a, an, the) used correctly?

____ ____ Are the forms of the words (verb, noun, adjective) used correctly?

____ ____ Are all the word choices appropriate?

____ ____ Are all the sentences in correct order?

Got It!
Sentence Order

Writing any kind of essay is a process. The most important part of that process is checking to make sure that readers can understand your message without difficulty. Therefore, the sentences in each paragraph of your essay must be in logical order. A paragraph from another process essay follows. Put the sentences into the correct order to explain the process. Number the sentences first, and then write a paragraph that shows the sentences in the correct order.

Do not cut the entire pizza before you begin to eat.

Enjoy!

Slowly slide the pizza onto a cutting board.

After the cheese on the top of the pizza is bubbling, it is time to take the pizza out of the oven.

Cutting it makes it get cold too fast, and cold pizza is not good.

After you let it cool briefly, cut it into pieces with a pizza cutter.

When everyone has been served, sit down with lots of napkins and a cool drink.

Got It!
Word Order in Individual Sentences

You want readers to understand your essays, so you know that you need to organize the sentences in each of your paragraphs in a logical order. It is just as important to be sure that the individual words in each of your sentences also follow a meaningful order. Sometimes when you change the placement of one word, you can change the meaning of the entire sentence. Look at the following groups of words. It is impossible to get any meaning from them in their present order. Rewrite each word group so that it forms a sentence that is clear and, therefore, easy for readers to understand.

1. can rent each how I month afford much

   _____

2. newspaper's the look section is homes place for easiest the to classified in

   _____

3. and lived old manager place the is or how who landlord previously there ask the

   _____

4. you sign need have you once lease to a will decided

   _____

5. before always lease the completely sign it read you

   _____

Peer Feedback Form

The following is a list of more elements to examine when you read a classmate's writing or your own. The list can be used as a short peer feedback form, or it can be used with the main Peer Feedback Form on page 63.

(CIRCLE ONE)

1. **True   False**   The writer used a variety of sequence signals.

2. **True   False**   The writer does not use only personal examples to support the ideas in the essay.

3. **True   False**   Some words in the essay look as if they are misspelled. Those words are: (Write the words as shown in the essay.)

   _____

   _____

   _____.

4.3 The Classification Essay

WHAT DOES IT DO?

- A **classification essay** introduces a primary category and then shows how three or more subtopics or members are related to that primary category.
- It clearly describes each subtopic and gives equal description to the way that each subtopic relates to the primary topic.
- Example: Primary Category: Transportation
  - Subtopics: Automobiles
    - Ships
    - Airplanes
    - Trains

WHAT DOES IT CONTAIN?

- A **classification essay** has an introductory paragraph that first talks about the primary topic and then separates the primary topic into three or more subtopics.
- Each body paragraph in this essay talks about one of the subtopics. There are clear transitions from one body paragraph to the next.
- This essay concludes with a paragraph that restates the thesis and brings the subtopics back to the primary category.

WHAT DOES IT DISCUSS?

A **classification essay** usually discusses members of a category. The members can be behaviors, people, ideas, or jobs. These are just some examples. Whatever the topics, the subtopics (members) all have to be the same type. For example, all three subtopics could be different persons who have something in common. However, a person, a room, and an event cannot be subtopics because they do not have an obvious, common relationship.

• SAMPLE CLASSIFICATION ESSAY •

Bosses

Whether you are about to begin your first job, or whether you are already an experienced employee, you know that when you have a job, you must work with someone who holds the title of "boss." It may be useful for you to know that bosses tend to fall into categories. While there are certainly overlaps and perhaps no one person can be or should be strictly labeled, in general they fall into groups according to the way they usually deal with problems. We can classify bosses as Problem Causers, Problem Evaders, and Problem Solvers.

With the apparent view that relationships between employers and employees will not cause enough problems naturally, Problem Causers need to ensure tense situations. For example, even though except for emergencies, their employees are responsible for arriving on time to their jobs each day, Problem Causers believe that the installation of a time clock will frighten any worker who might be tempted to take advantage of the "honor system" and lapse into intentional lateness. Wearing clothing appropriate to the job is not normally a problem for employees who take their job seriously. As with the time clock installation, Problem Causers need to establish dress codes "just in case." Problem Causers like to state the obvious, so they like to remind their workers of such things as, "The lunch hour means sixty minutes," "You need to call me if you're sick and can't come to work," and "Not all of you can take your vacation at the same time." If a worker needs to be reprimanded for a legitimate violation,

Don't like problems (handwritten marginal note)

get mad (handwritten note at bottom)

— yet like your the
parents to a
child.

Problem Causers like to scold this person in a more or less public location. The scolding can take place at the employee's work station with others uncomfortably pretending to be deaf, in the Problem Causer's office with the door open, or sometimes even in the restroom, where the employee is probably going to feel vulnerable and embarrassed. To be one hundred percent certain of their positions, Problem Causers have been heard to remind their employees, "Don't forget who's the boss here."

The exact opposite of Problem Causers are those of the Problem Evaders group. While there is nothing wrong with giving some authority to subordinates, Problem Evaders actually give as many of their own responsibilities as they can to other people. Problem Evaders are uncomfortable with conflict, so it is not surprising that they avoid eye contact when an employee approaches them with a problem. They then suggest that one of their subordinates is the person who normally handles that particular kind of situation. When it is time to discuss annual raises, Problem Evaders give the task to a subordinate even though they themselves make the final decision. They use this system to escape the "bad guy" image if workers' pay increases do not meet their expectations. Problem Evaders use physical means to evade work problems as well. Because getting a gym membership is many times a benefit of the top job, taking work time to go play volleyball is certainly, to those left behind, a way to avoid work itself as well as any problems that may arise during the absence. Problem Evaders are entitled to use every hour, day, and week of vacation that their job is promised, of course. Arriving at work early before anyone else so that they "can leave early to avoid heavy traffic," however, seems like a very clever type of evasion. In the early morning with no one else yet in the work place, it is quite unlikely that employee problems will arise and need to be dealt with. By the time the day gets started and problems demand attention, it is, "Oh, I'm so sorry, but can you talk to someone else? I've already put in my day." Once again, a person who doesn't receive the pay, the benefits, or the title of boss gets stuck with the boss's responsibility.

When workers are lucky, they don't get the Problem Causer or the Problem Evader; instead they work for Problem Solvers. Problem Solvers are not too busy to deal with employee difficulties. If the difficulties cannot be taken care of immediately, Problem Solvers suggest a time and place for further discussion as soon as possible. Problem Solvers are excellent listeners. They can't always fill requests for position changes, pay increases, or time-off, but they listen to those requests and either act on them if they can, or explain the reasons if they cannot. Problem Solvers are creative thinkers, so they are skilled at offering alternative solutions to problems, usually beginning their suggestion with, "What do you think about . . . ?" or "What if we tried . . . ?" Problem Solvers are fair. It is possible that not all their employees are equally skilled in all tasks. Problem Solvers try to observe and make use of the strengths of each individual in order to create feelings of satisfaction and achievement for the persons as well as for the group and to discourage bitter competition. Problem Solvers have a sense of humor about themselves. Remembering that anyone can make a mistake, they are not embarrassed to admit when they do, and they can relieve tension by making jokes about themselves.

It would be useless to wish that only Problem Solvers could rise to the top levels in their job because the reality is that the Problem Causers and Problem Evaders get those positions too. Whether through family connections, collecting on obligations of friends, successfully disguising their true personalities, or plain old luck, there is a chance that everyone will work for one of these negative types at some time. If you do, your choices are clear: you can quit, you can continue in spite of your boss, or you can decide to become a Problem Solver boss yourself.

EXAMINING THE CLASSIFICATION ESSAY

A **classification essay** takes a primary topic and divides it into three or four subtopics that are of equal importance.

This sample essay begins by personalizing the topic of bosses. Then the writer narrows the topic into three subtopics which are called types of bosses. Those types of bosses lead into the following thesis statement: *We can classify bosses as Problem Causers, Problem Evaders, and Problem Solvers.* The reader knows that the writer will discuss each of these subtopics individually in the body of the essay.

Your Turn!

Answer the following questions about *Bosses* in order to understand the **classification essay** and how it was constructed.

1. Why does the writer call the first type of boss a Problem Causer?
2. Describe a Problem Evader.
3. Why is the Problem Solver the best kind of boss?

WRITE!

When you choose your topics for a **classification essay,** you need to think about a general topic that you know very well and that can be divided into three or four subtopics with two or more specific examples for each of those subtopics. There is no limit to the number of subtopics you can choose. Just remember that each subtopic must have its own body paragraph. The details in the body paragraphs make your essay strong.

Look at another **classification essay** on page 155! Can you identify the three subtopics in that essay? Now try writing one yourself!

If you're having trouble thinking of a topic, here are some ideas for a **classification essay.**

- types of vacations
- people who have influenced me
- places I like to spend time
- activities I do not enjoy
- free activities that are fun to do
- favorite objects from my childhood

Checklist for a Classification Essay

CONTENT

GOOD OK NEEDS WORK

____ ____ ____ The essay discusses a primary topic from which at least three subtopics can be formed.

____ ____ ____ The essay explains each of the three subtopics and shows how they are related to the primary topic.

____ ____ ____ The essay gives equal description or examples for each of the three subtopics.

____ ____ ____ The essay uses "word pictures" to show the subtopics.

ORGANIZATION

GOOD OK NEEDS WORK

____ ____ ____ The introductory paragraph leads from a primary topic into at least three subtopics.

____ ____ ____ The thesis statement states the subtopics and their relationship to the primary topic.

____ ____ ____ Each body paragraph begins with a topic sentence.

____ ____ ____ Each paragraph of the body clearly describes one of the three subtopics.

____ ____ ____ The body paragraphs connect to each other with transition words or phrases.

____ ____ ____ The concluding paragraph restates the thesis and brings the subtopics back to their primary topic.

MECHANICS

YES NO

____ ____ Does each sentence have a subject, a verb, and a complete thought?

____ ____ Does each sentence begin with a capital letter and end with a period?

____ ____ Do all the word combinations (subject-verb, adjective-noun, noun-pronoun) agree with each other?

____ ____ Does the verb tense express the appropriate time in each sentence?

____ ____ Are all the words spelled correctly?

____ ____ Are the articles (a, an, the) used correctly?

____ ____ Are the forms of the words (verb, noun, adjective) used correctly?

____ ____ Are all the word choices appropriate?

____ ____ Are all the sentences in correct order?

Got It!
Show, Not Tell: Word Pictures

Definitions **tell** what words mean, but *word pictures* **show** the meaning of a word through the use of concrete examples. When you create "word pictures," readers can "see" in their imaginations exactly what you are describing or explaining. These word pictures are especially effective when they are used to support and clarify why a writer has chosen certain words for descriptions of people or events. For example, a writer can make a vivid word picture by **showing** a person in action, using both the person's deeds and the person's exact words.

The classification essay about types of bosses clearly illustrates the concept of *word pictures.* The writer shows the actions of each **type** of boss and quotes a typical statement or question from each type.

Look at the Bosses essay and answer the following questions.

1. What are some of the actions of the Problem Causer boss?
   What is a typical quote from the Problem Causer boss?
2. What are some of the actions of the Problem Evader boss?
   What is a typical quote from the Problem Evader boss?
3. What are some of the actions of a Problem Solver boss?
   What is a typical quote from the Problem Solver boss?

Your Turn!

Now you try it with the descriptions below. **Do not write a definition.** Write a sentence showing each of these people in an action that would clarify why the adjective is a good choice for that person. Then write something that each of these people might say that would further support the adjective. (For examples, look at your answers in the Got It! section.)

1. **a generous woman**

   Your sentence showing this woman in a specific **generous** action:

   _____

   Your sentence with a typical quotation from this **generous** woman:

   _____

2. **a jealous boyfriend/girlfriend**

   Your sentence showing the boyfriend/girlfriend in a specific **jealous** action:

   _____

   Your sentence with a typical quotation from this **jealous** boyfriend/
   girlfriend:

   _____

3. **a lazy brother or a lazy sister**

   Your sentence showing this brother or sister in a specific **lazy** action:

   _____

   Your sentence with a typical quotation from this **lazy** brother or sister:

   _____

Peer Feedback Form

The following is a list of more elements to examine when you read a classmate's writing or your own. The list can be used as a short peer feedback form, or it can be used with the main Peer Feedback Form on page 63.

(CIRCLE ONE)

1. **True   False**   There is sentence variety in this writing. Some sentences are

                          simple, but others are compound or complex.*

                          *A compound sentence is a combination of two sentences with a conjunction like *and, or,* **or** *but*. **A complex sentence uses transition phrases like** *because, if,* **and** *although*. **Both compound and complex sentences may also have special punctuation inside the sentences in order to allow for their length, for example, commas or semicolons.**

2. **True   False**   The writer used the correct verb tense consistently. It was clear

                          when the writer was talking about the present and talking

                          about the past or the future.

3.   Does the writer use one phrase or word repetitively throughout the essay?

     If yes, what is that word or phrase? _____

4.4 The Comparison/Contrast Essay

WHAT DOES IT DO?

- A **comparison/contrast essay** shows essential similarities (comparison) or differences (contrast) between two items with a basic relationship.
- It provides equal details about both items discussed.

WHAT DOES IT CONTAIN?

- A **comparison/contrast essay** has a beginning paragraph that introduces the relationship between the items to be discussed.
- This essay has a thesis statement that names both items and states whether the writer will talk about similarities or about differences.
- Each body paragraph of this essay discusses separate similarities or differences in detail for both topics.
- This essay has a concluding paragraph that restates the thesis and brings the topics back together.

WHAT DOES IT DISCUSS?

- A **comparison essay** talks about two items that seem different but that are actually very similar.
- A **contrast essay** usually talks about two items that seem similar but that are actually quite different.

Comparison/Contrast Organization
OUTLINE 1
(The model comparison essay that follows emphasizes similarities.)

TOPIC A	TOPIC B
being a teacher	being a tour guide

Introduction: Writer introduces the idea of choosing a career.

Body Paragraph 1:   Topic A and Topic B Similarities
a. training and preparation for Topic A
b. training and preparation for Topic B

Body Paragraph 2:   Topic A and Topic B Similarities
a. management and problems for Topic A
b. management and problems for Topic B

Conclusion

• SAMPLE COMPARISON ESSAY •

Classroom or Bus?

If you are considering a career that offers constant contact with interesting people, the daily opportunity of discussing your favorite topics, and a chance to enrich the lives of others, you might consider either becoming a secondary school teacher or becoming a tour director. Standing at the front of a classroom talking about history and literature to forty adolescents, or standing at the front of a bus explaining landmarks or historical sites to forty adults might seem to be careers with little in common. When these jobs are carefully examined, however, striking similarities between the two quickly surface.

The preparation for each career is similar, both long and short term. To become teachers, students must first complete a university program with a major in the area they plan to teach. Following this program, they are required to put theory into practice by teaching real students in real settings under the leadership of an experienced teacher who serves as supervisor. This student-teaching setting is where prospective teachers first learn about the importance of specific lesson preparation. Students, particularly adolescents, can take joy in "catching the teacher" in a mistake or asking a question designed to divert the teacher from the topic of the lesson. They also tend to be quite perceptive in recognizing when teachers are bluffing or when they are not well enough prepared to keep a lesson on track, so it is wise to be ready for anything. Unlike teachers, tour guides are not required to have a university degree, although many of them do. A comprehensive study of the history of the area where they want to work is crucial. Furthermore, they may need to revisit many places to familiarize themselves with museums and other sites. In contrast to adolescents, adults usually do not try to catch another person making a mistake, but many of those on the tour bus are very knowledgeable themselves, and several of them will have learned many details about the area they are traveling. Consequently their questions, while usually polite and sincere, can upset the tour guide who has not prepared for the specific itinerary of each day's tour.

Management skills, too, are similar in teaching and tour guiding. From the routine of physical arrangement to the strictly set time schedule, both teachers and guides face challenges. Forty students with forty desks presents no problem, providing the classroom is composed of forty angelically cooperative adolescent souls. Keeping physical as well as verbal conflicts to a minimum is closer to reality. Add to these difficulties the simple problems of time management. A prescribed number of pages per day, chapters per week, and books per semester can be challenging to complete, even without the interruptions of bathroom breaks, fire or bomb scare drills, school assemblies, or any surprise unscheduled event. Similarly, the tour guide must deal with management problems. Again, forty adults, forty seats, no problem, providing the bus is filled with forty unselfish cooperative adult individuals. Unfortunately, some positions on the bus are superior to others: window or aisle, back or front, not to mention proximity to the exits for brief bathroom and/or lunch breaks. Like teachers, tour guides must follow a rigid agenda, theirs with a specific number of miles to be covered each day, timely stops for lunches, an attempt at late afternoon arrival for each hotel stay, and probably most difficult of all, early departures for the following day, usually each and every day of a tour.

Being well prepared and managing difficult situations and schedules with unlimited patience are all requirements for happy and successful teachers and tour guides. If you are trying to decide which career is right for you, you might think carefully about these similarities. If you want to simplify your decision, ask yourself whether you prefer to go to a familiar work location each day, or if you would like a constantly changing work location. You can be sure that either career offers many rich rewards.

Comparison/Contrast Organization
OUTLINE 2
(The following model contrast essay emphasizes differences.)

TOPIC A   **TOPIC B**
studying a new language in your country   studying a language abroad

Introduction: Writer introduces the idea of studying a language, recognizes a few similarities between learning a language domestically and abroad, states differences in general.

Body Paragraph 1: **Topic A**
a. living conditions
b. food
c. friends
d. using money
e. getting around
f. legal situations

Body Paragraph 2: **Topic A**
a. types of fellow students
b. teaching methods
c. language(s) used in class
d. socializing with classmates

Body Paragraph 3: **Topic B**
a. living conditions
b. food
c. friends
d. using money
e. getting around
f. legal situations

Body Paragraph 4: **Topic B**
a. types of fellow students
b. teaching methods
c. language(s) used in class
d. socializing with classmates

Conclusion

SAMPLE CONTRAST ESSAY

At Home or Abroad?

Learning a language in addition to your own native language enriches your life, but it takes commitment. Once you have decided that you are willing to spend the effort to master another language, you will need to make some important decisions regarding where and how you want to learn it. It is obvious that going to another country to study the language requires more money than staying at home attending a local language school in your own city. If cost is not your primary concern, however, you will want to think hard about other differences between learning a language in your own country or going abroad to study.

If you choose to stay in your country to study a new language, you will be able to sleep in your own bed each night, eat all the food you love, and have your favorite possessions near at hand. After a day or week at school if you decide to have an unscheduled party, you can call friends who probably can join you in a matter of minutes. When you need spending money for movies, restaurants, or other entertainment expenses, either you have some saved from a job or you have an agreement with your parents, so all you have to do is get the cash and go. If you want to buy clothes, you know the best places to shop and the approximate cost you will have to pay. If anyone tries to overcharge, you are instantly aware of the plan to cheat you. You know how to travel wherever you want to go in your own city and which neighborhoods tend to be dangerous. If you have any legal business such as getting a driver's license or signing a contract, or maybe even paying a traffic violation fine, you understand exactly what is expected of you.

In language class, too, you probably won't have many surprises. You might even have known some of your fellow students from before the first class meeting. Maybe your teachers are from a country that uses the language you are studying and are therefore "native speakers", but it is almost certainly true that they speak your language as well. Because you and all the other students, and the teachers, share the same language, many of the class explanations and vocabulary can be translated directly to you in your native language. The teachers may remind you to speak only in the "foreign" language, but they and you know that it is much easier to use your own, especially at the beginning levels of language study. You might decide that all you need to do is put a new set of vocabulary words into the grammar system you have been using all your life. During the class breaks you and the other students will chatter away in your native language because you will feel a relief at being able to talk fast and fluently after struggling during the class lessons. You will surely make new friends from the classes and it will be easy to continue your relationships with them even after you have all completed your language study.

If you decide instead to go to a foreign country to study the language, your new bed will be in the home of a host family, in a hotel, or maybe in a dormitory room. The food will be typical of the country and not what you are accustomed to at home. If you want to get together with friends from home, you can, but it will have to be by expensive telephone calls, "snail" letter mail, or by e-mail. Either you will need to budget all your money, both for fun and for necessity, or you will need credit card privileges from your family. When you go shopping, you will have to calculate constantly what the cost is in "real" money, your home currency. You will need to be continuously on the watch for dishonest money-handlers who might take advantage of your ignorance of the system. Using public transportation or driving in an unfamiliar city can be frustrating and even risky if you wander into the wrong areas. If you try to get a driver's license or rent a car or an apartment, you will probably want to get a trusted "native" speaker to explain the legal language.

Going into your first classroom may be quite startling. There might be a few people from your country, but probably there will be a mixture instead; in a class of only ten people, six or seven countries and languages could be represented. All your teachers will be "native" speakers and even if they also know your first language, they will not use it in the classroom. In general, you can forget any teacher translation. With many other languages represented in the class it probably would not even be possible, but more importantly, the basic concept of learning a new language is learning to think in that language. There may be grammatical similarities between your language and the one you are studying, but they are not identical and often trying to construct a sentence with your own grammar can produce unintentionally amusing results. Those other students in the classroom are just as eager as you for break time, but if you want to get your money's worth for your lessons, you can learn much more if you promise yourself to speak only with people who are not from your country. Not only will you learn more, but you can also develop international friendships. Once your language study is finished and you return home, you will have the possibility of continuing friendships worldwide with these other students, often by e-mail, but sometimes by actual visits to their countries during some future time in your life.

There is no question that learning a language at home is cheaper and less stressful than studying abroad, but the experiences that accompany the latter are the most important differences. Being away from your familiar way of life forces you to be self-reliant, and it truly opens the doors of the world. Even the names of the learning systems point up a very important distinction; in your own country, it is called "foreign" language study, but abroad it is known as "second" language learning. Whichever method you choose will require your dedication if you sincerely want to master another language.

EXAMINING THE COMPARISON/CONTRAST ESSAY

The first sample essay in this section is a comparison essay. (See page 84.) It takes two basically related topics and points out the likenesses. The second sample essay is a contrast essay. (See page 88.) It takes two topics that have a basic commonality and points out the differences between the topics.

This sample **contrast essay** considers two different ways of studying a foreign language. The introduction acknowledges that cost is an obvious difference between the two ways and then leads to this thesis, *If cost is not your primary concern, however, you will want to think hard about other differences between learning a language in your own country or going abroad to study.* The body paragraphs state and explain those differences.

There are two basic forms of organization for the **comparison** or **contrast essays.**

> **OUTLINE 1:** One point is discussed as it relates to both topics, and then another point is discussed as it relates to both topics, and so on. (See page 84.)
>
> **OUTLINE 2:** All the points of one topic are discussed, and then all the corresponding points of the other topic are discussed. (See page 87.)

 ## Your Turn!

Answer the following questions about *At Home or Abroad?* in order to understand the **contrast essay** and how it was constructed.

1. What are the major points of contrast in the first body paragraph? What is one detail of those points?
2. What is the main point of contrast in the next body paragraph? What is one detail?
3. The third paragraph of the body covers the same points as the first paragraph of the body. What is the detail that corresponds to your detail from Question 1?
4. The fourth paragraph corresponds to the same points as the second paragraph of the body. What is the detail that corresponds to your detail from Question 2?

WRITE!

When you are deciding what to choose for a **comparison/contrast essay** topic, you need to think about topics that are basically related but that have distinct, although not obvious, differences or similarities.

Look at another comparison/contrast essay on page 159. Then try writing one yourself!

   If you're having trouble thinking of a topic, here are some ideas for a **comparison/contrast essay.**

- going to a movie/going to a concert
- working as a police officer/working as a soldier
- playing sports as an athlete/watching sports as a spectator
- living in a future outer space community/living in a future underwater community
- dating someone from your own culture/dating someone from a different culture
- getting information from the television/getting information from reading

Checklist for a Comparison/Contrast Essay

CONTENT

GOOD OK **NEEDS WORK**

____ ____ ____   The essay compares and/or contrasts two related topics.

____ ____ ____   The essay stresses either similarities or differences of its two topics.

____ ____ ____   The essay provides equal details and examples for both topics.

____ ____ ____   The essay uses "word pictures" to show the similarities/differences.

ORGANIZATION

GOOD OK **NEEDS WORK**

____ ____ ____   The introductory paragraph shows a basic relationship between the two topics and leads to a thesis statement.

____ ____ ____   The thesis statement names both of the topics and states clearly whether the emphasis will be on the similarities or on the differences.

____ ____ ____   Each body paragraph begins with a topic sentence.

____ ____ ____   The essay shows corresponding differences or similarities of both topics in each of the body paragraphs.

____ ____ ____   The essay uses transition words or phrases to connect the two topics.

____ ____ ____   The essay concludes with a restatement of the thesis and reference to the differences or the similarities between the two topics.

MECHANICS

YES   NO

____ ____   Does each sentence have a subject, a verb, and a complete thought?

____ ____   Does each sentence begin with a capital letter and end with a period?

____ ____   Do all the word combinations (subject-verb, adjective-noun, noun-pronoun) agree with each other?

____ ____   Does the verb tense express the appropriate time in each sentence?

____ ____   Are all the words spelled correctly?

____ ____   Are the articles (a, an, the) used correctly?

____ ____   Are the forms of the words (verb, noun, adjective) used correctly?

____ ____   Are all the word choices appropriate?

____ ____   Are all the sentences in correct order?

Got It!
Balanced Topics Exercise

When you select main topics for a comparison/contrast essay, it is necessary to think about the possible problems of balancing the two things/people you want to compare or contrast before you begin your essay. First you need to subdivide your possible main topics into at least three elements (subtopics) that you wish to compare or contrast. Then you need to be sure that you can think of an equal number of details or examples for each of your subtopics. Once you can see that your main topics can be balanced, you are ready to begin writing your essay. Here are two exercises that will help show you how to ensure that your topics will be of equal importance.

Fill in possible subtopics and a few words of detail or example for these main topics.

TOPIC A: **a weekend at a resort**   TOPIC B: **a weekend of camping**
          hotel

SUBTOPIC 1
weather at night

DETAILS   DETAILS
warm Hotell   _cold in a tent_
Room comfortable bed   _with sleeping bags_

SUBTOPIC 2
bathrooms

DETAILS   DETAILS   _, dirty_
clean bath rooms   _public bathroms_
with hot water   _only cold water_ _th_

SUBTOPIC 3
Food

DETAILS   DETAILS
Hotel Restorant,   _Barbiqued food_
and room service   _and call samwiches_

Do the same with these main topics.

TOPIC A: **your mother**   TOPIC B: **your father**

SUBTOPIC 1

persenalty

DETAILS   DETAILS

stricts   *very frendly*
                                 and easy

SUBTOPIC 2

aut going

DETAILS   DETAILS

like going aut trips   *likes to stay*
for camping   *home and watch*
                                 movies

SUBTOPIC 3

_____

DETAILS   DETAILS

_____   _____
_____   _____

Peer Feedback Form

The following is a list of more elements to examine when you read a classmate's writing or your own. The list can be used as a short peer feedback form, or it can be used with the main Peer Feedback Form on page 63.

(CIRCLE ONE)

1. **True   False**   Every sentence has a subject and a verb.*

   ***If a sentence does not have both a subject and a verb, it is a *fragment*. A fragment is part of a sentence, not a whole sentence. Read more about fragments on page 128 in Unit 5.**

2. **True   False**   The writer correctly uses plural quantifiers (*many, some, a lot, a few*) with plural nouns and singular quantifiers with singular nouns.

3. **True   False**   I learned something from this essay that I did not know before I read it.

   Example: _____

4.5 The Cause and Effect Essay

WHAT DOES IT DO?

- A **cause and effect essay** shows the causal relationship between two items/concepts. It uses concrete examples to show a direct relationship between specific causes and their one effect.
- It could also show the relationship between one cause and its effects.
- It convincingly shows the relationship between an effect and its causes or a cause and its effects.

WHAT DOES IT CONTAIN?

- A **cause and effect essay** has a general introduction leading to a thesis statement that indicates a direct link between stated cause(s) and effect(s).
- All body paragraphs must discuss all effects or all causes. Each body paragraph is devoted to one individual cause or effect.
- This essay concludes with a thesis restatement and a summary of the relationship between the cause(s) and the effect(s).

WHAT DOES IT DISCUSS?

- A **cause and effect essay** discusses the different causes after it briefly discusses the common effect.

  or

- A **cause and effect essay** discusses the different effects of one common cause.

• SAMPLE CAUSE AND EFFECT ESSAY •

Body Language around the World

An American foreign exchange student studying Portuguese in Brazil was having a weekly lesson with his Brazilian teacher. The teacher had just finished a long, complicated explanation of a grammar point, so she asked her student if he understood what she had just said. Still a little shaky in Portuguese, the man responded with body language. He smiled and put the tips of his thumb and forefinger together to form a circle, the American gesture for "O.K." The teacher's eyes widened in disbelief. She gasped, stood up, and stomped out of the classroom, never to return. The American was bewildered. Little did he know that he had just made a very lewd gesture to the woman. Body language, and particularly gestures, can be just as different from country to country as spoken languages, and more particularly, just as important. Understanding and using gestures which are used in the host country can prevent misunderstood messages, reflect your fluency in that country's language and culture, and for business people, such knowledge can ensure business success.

Inappropriate gestures, or in some cases, any gesture at all, can send unintended messages and in some cases, do irreparable damage to a relationship. In Roger Axtell's book *Gestures: The Do's and Taboos of Body Language around the World*, the author tells of an incident in which public affection by a foreigner was seen as a crime in the host country.

"An American woman gets into a car with an American man, slides over to his side, and kisses him on the cheek.

A common enough occurrence that probably happens
hundreds of thousands of times each day in the United
States. But in this case, it happened to be in Saudi Arabia
where public displays of affection are disliked, even forbidden, and marriage is sacrosanct. The woman was sent out
of the country and the man, who compounded his problem by being argumentative, was sent to jail." (pp. 8–9,
*Gestures, the Do's and Taboos of Body Language around the
World,* Roger E. Axtell, 1998, John Wiley & Sons, Inc.)

In this case, as in the one mentioned above, a misunderstanding
is a common occurrence when one of the participants is not familiar with what his/her gesture means in the host country. One
gesture may be translated as a sign of friendliness whereas the
same gesture, in another country, may be viewed as a personal
expression of lust or desire.

Gestures also reflect a person's respect for the culture and his
fluency in a language. The more a non-native speaker's spoken
fluency in a second language improves, the more he will be expected by native speakers to acquiesce to other parts of the culture, namely the body language. In other words, native speakers
may be more likely to forgive a beginning speaker of a *faux pas* in
gestures, but they may not be so understanding if a near-native
foreign speaker makes the same mistake. In addition, if one is
truly learning the language of the host country, he would be ig-
norant and disrespectful if he merely learned the grammar and
the vocabulary and disregarded the gestures of that language.
After all, many words are expressed with gestures. For business
people in Japan or Korea, simultaneous to or immediately
following the first greeting, business cards are exchanged and

then kept face-up, in plain sight until the meeting is over. In Indochina, if a native male from that area were walking with his American male friend down the street and suddenly grabbed the hand of his American friend, the two might get barely five steps down the street hand-in-hand when the American man would shake off his hand and tell his host, "I'm not gay." This is the way a visitor, in this case, an American, could insult his host's kind intentions because he might not know that in the Middle East, China, and Indochina, hand-holding between males is a sign of true friendship. Foreign guests have an obligation to learn about the gestures of a country and to respect and understand them as much as they can.

For business people and politicians, too, impressing hosts, clients, or buyers with appropriate gestures is a great way to break the ice, but more importantly, it is a great way to show respect for that country's unwritten rules. Appropriate gestures reflect on the businessman and his company. Take, for example, the simplest of meeting tasks, the handshake. Is it really so simple? Even in America, parents and teachers give varying advice on how to shake hands at the first interview, or when meeting a girlfriend/ boyfriend's parents. In some countries, there is no such thing as a handshake at all. The Maori people of New Zealand greet each other by rubbing their noses together. In Japan, people bow deeply to each other and shake hands at the same time. In Germany, however, people love to shake hands when greeting, when leaving on a trip, when coming back, and even on non-social occasions. Sometimes, the handshake is accompanied by other gestures. For example, in Bolivia, friends shake hands and then slap each other on the back. Certainly, the handshake or the initial greeting creates the first impression of the businessperson, the business itself, and the level of respect demanded of that organization. A good first impression will usually ensure a successful business transaction.

A lack of knowledge of appropriate body language and gestures of the host country can result in bad business deals and in embarrassing and sometimes awkward situations. The same gesture can have completely different usage and connotation in each culture/country. Knowing and using these gestures is not only a sign of respect for the host country, but it is also a reflection of your true fluency in the language of that country, both physical and verbal languages.

EXAMINING THE CAUSE AND EFFECT ESSAY

A **cause and effect essay** shows a direct relationship between specific actions and their specific results. One kind of **cause and effect essay** will discuss one cause and its many effects. Another kind of **cause and effect essay** will discuss an effect and its many causes.

In this sample essay, a detailed anecdote about an unfortunate cultural misunderstanding brings us to the thesis statement, *Understanding and using gestures which are used in the host country can prevent misunderstood messages, reflect your fluency in that country's language and culture, and for business people, such knowledge can ensure business success.* The essay continues with examples that show the three effects that result from the stated cause.

Your Turn!

Answer the following questions about *Body Language around the World* in order to understand the **cause and effect essay** and how it is constructed.

1. What is the misunderstood message in the first paragraph of the body?
2. What is an example of a misunderstood gesture in the second body paragraph?
3. From the third body paragraph, what are two different types of greetings that an international businessperson should know about?

WRITE!

With a **cause and effect** essay, you need to choose a topic that has very strong connections from result(s) back to action(s) or from action(s) to cause(s). Your purpose is to make those connections seem logical to your reader.

Look at another **cause and effect essay** on page 163! How would you have written this essay differently? Now write your own **cause and effect essay**!

If you're having trouble thinking of a topic, here are some ideas for a **cause/effect essay.**

- arranged marriages
- making a major career change
- overweight children
- industrial pollution
- drugs in sports
- downloading music from the Internet

Checklist for a Cause and Effect Essay

CONTENT

GOOD OK NEEDS WORK

____ ____ ____   The essay discusses a causal relationship between two items or concepts.

____ ____ ____   The essay shows a direct link betweenthe cause(s) and effect(s) with concrete examples.

____ ____ ____   The essay makes a convincing link between cause(s) and effect(s).

____ ____ ____   The essay uses "word pictures" to show the cause(s) and effect(s).

ORGANIZATION

GOOD OK NEEDS WORK

____ ____ ____   The introductory paragraph leads to a thesis statement that indicates a direct link between stated cause and effect.

____ ____ ____   Each paragraph in the body begins with a topic sentence.

____ ____ ____   Each body paragraph shows a convincing relationship between cause and effect with specific details and support.

____ ____ ____   The body paragraphs connect to each other with transition words or phrases.

____ ____ ____   The concluding paragraph persuasively restates the thesis and summarizes the examples in the body paragraphs.

MECHANICS

YES NO

____ ____   Does each sentence have a subject, a verb, and a complete thought?

____ ____   Does each sentence begin with a capital letter and end with a period?

____ ____   Do all the word combinations (subject-verb, adjective-noun, noun-pronoun) agree with each other?

____ ____   Does the verb tense express the appropriate time in each sentence?

____ ____   Are all the words spelled correctly?

____ ____   Are the articles *(a, an, the)* used correctly?

____ ____   Are the forms of the words (verb, noun, adjective) used correctly?

____ ____   Are all the word choices appropriate?

____ ____   Are all the sentences in correct order?

Got It!
Going from Cause to Effect

When you are writing a cause and effect essay, you need to explain the direct results that you believe come from a specific cause. For example, one writer believes that the Internet has some negative aspects, so the cause and effect essay contains several examples of <u>negative</u> results of using the Internet. In the body of the essay, one of the topic sentences is: **E-mail has replaced letter writing and casual telephoning.** Obviously, this statement is a fact. People who regularly use the Internet for e-mail agree that they do not write as many paper-and-pen letters or contact friends by phone as much as they did before they had e-mail. The challenge is to show why this replacement of letter writing and casual telephoning by e-mail is <u>negative</u>. How many examples can you think of? List them below.

_____

_____

_____

Now read the actual paragraph from the essay. Did you have any of the same negative examples as this writer?

E-mail has replaced letter writing and casual telephoning. Because we have daily access to home and business computers, it has become more convenient to send off a quick e-mail rather than to pick up the telephone and have a conversation. Handwriting a letter on a card or stationery has become almost obsolete as we have become accustomed to the fast and easy system of punching out an e-mail and with a quick push of a button, sending it anywhere in the world. As a result, the relationships we have with each other have become more superficial, convenience-oriented, and short-lived. Through a phone call, we can hear each other's voices, pick up on hurt feelings, worry, or stress through the pace of speech, the pauses in conversation, the laughter, or the weeping. In a written letter, we are more likely to share family news, and our emotions emerge through the message on the card, the choice of paper, the complexity of the sentence, or in our handwriting. More importantly, letters cannot be lost in cyberspace or deleted automatically after seven days. Letters last forever; the ink, the stamps, and the language serve as lessons about a specific era in history. A recent advertisement for one of the largest telecommunications companies in America illustrates the story of a dad who places a long-distance call to his daughter because her e-mail is confusing and vague. He says he needs to hear her voice to find out what is really "going on." Further evidence of the prevalence of e-mail can be seen by the current financial status of the United States Post Office, which is now in billions of dollars of debt and temporarily halting all hiring. E-mail has become a quick substitute that is slowly killing the practice of letter-writing and casual phone calls.

Peer Feedback Form

The following is a list of more elements to examine when you read a classmate's writing or your own. The list can be used as a short peer feedback form, or it can be used with the main Peer Feedback Form on page 63.

(CIRCLE ONE)

1. **True   False**   There are no sentences that start with **so**.*

      ***Using *so* as a conjunction requires that *so* be placed between an effect and a cause, so the two parts of an idea are connected in one sentence.**

2. **True   False**   The writer does not use double negatives.**

      ****Double negatives are two negative words put together to form an idea. The problem is that, just as in mathematics, two negatives make a positive. This means that double negatives are not effective negative expressions. An example of a double negative would be: *I don't have nothing*. This actually means: *I have something*.**

3. **True   False**   All of the sentences are punctuated correctly.

4.6 The Persuasion Essay

WHAT DOES IT DO?

- A **persuasion essay** forcefully states an opinion on an issue/belief.
- It has logical compelling anecdotes, factual reports, and other examples to support the opinion in the thesis statement.
- It works hard to make the reader agree with the writer and/or to make the reader understand and accept a different point of view.
- It evokes strong emotions, but its arguments are based on reason.

WHAT DOES IT CONTAIN?

- A **persuasion essay** has a thesis statement that clearly states the opinion to be expressed in the essay. (The introductory paragraph also recognizes, but does not discuss in depth, opposing opinions.)
- Each paragraph in the body provides detailed support for the thesis statement.
- This essay concludes with a restatement of the opinion and a summary of the arguments.

WHAT DOES IT DISCUSS?

A **persuasion essay** is also sometimes called a **position paper.** It usually discusses one side of a controversial issue. It is a very strong essay because it discusses clear, logical arguments without emotion. A persuasion essay is often used on an essay exam when you are asked whether you agree or disagree with a controversial statement.

• SAMPLE PERSUASION ESSAY •

Arguments against Entrance Exams

The greatest stress for high school seniors all over the world is the university entrance exam. In America, it is the SAT and the ACT; in France, the baccalaureate and in Korea, the Soohak Nuenyuk Sheehum. Teens in nations all over the world spend most of their junior high and high school careers preparing, not for college or further study, but more particularly, for the entrance exam that is their only key to higher study. Does a student's performance on this test determine his success later in life, the kind of worker he will become, or the level of study he will complete? Does it ensure a successful college life? The answer to all of these questions is a resounding, "No!" Not only are traditional university entrance exams impractical and ineffective, but also they cause undue amounts of stress on the test-takers. Accordingly, such tests should be abolished.

The format and many of the items tested on the entrance exams are irrelevant to real life. The majority of entrance exams test language, in most cases, literature, and mathematics. Non-English speaking countries also might include an English as a Foreign Language section on the test. The English vocabulary tested on many of the exams includes words like *crepuscle, muzzy,* and *withy;* words which are rarely if ever used by most native or non-native speakers. The tests often require students to find synonyms or to define the words. Neither of these testing methods tests the students' ability to communicate orally or in written form. How well can these students organize their ideas? How concisely can they convey a message? How appropriately do they use the vocabulary or distinguish between words in written and spoken language? None of these questions is answered by the test although the skills referred to in each are relevant, necessary skills for success in a university classroom and in the workplace. Additionally, it is debatable what relevance mathematics has to a student who wishes to major in philosophy, music, or political science.

Scores on these languages and mathematics exams do not effectively predict student performance in the university. There are some students, who despite poor performance on class homework and presentations, or with poor attendance, can still perform well on multiple-choice items. Some students, despite their natural intelligence and high IQ's, are lazy, uninterested, and even disruptive in the classroom. Still other students who perform extremely well in class are prone to do well on essay-style exams rather than on multiple-choice tests. For all of these students, an entrance exam will be unable to predict their performance once they reach a university. Furthermore, academic achievement in the areas tested does not ensure social and psychological adaptation to university life and work. It seems strange that institutions of higher learning, often expensive and prestigious, would base their decision of admissions so greatly on one test because the test cannot distinguish between students who would contribute to the school and those who would merely feed off the school.

Seeing these tests as the only way to enter the university and thus to lead a middle to upper middle-class existence, students often suffer mental and physical anguish in preparing, taking, and coping with the outcomes of university entrance exams. In Japan and Korea, the rate of teen suicide increases dramatically in the fall each year at which time the university exams are given. Students, terrified that they will fail the exam or merely perform poorly and get admitted to a low-ranking university, and thus bring shame upon their family, jump from high-rise apartment buildings or hang themselves. In Korea, it is commonly said that the student who sleeps three hours a night will pass the exam, and the one who sleeps four will fail. In the United States, students are pressured to do well on exams like the SAT and the ACT, but at least they will also be judged on extra-curricular activities, community involvement, leadership roles, and grade point averages, as part of the admissions process. Unfortunately, in many other countries the exam is the only criteria for entrance. Stress-related illness, eating disorders, and sleep deprivation are all common ailments for the student whose only path to socially acceptable success is through the entrance exam.

The concept of basing entrance to a university on a single exam is, despite its strong history, obviously becoming irrelevant. Generally, the exams, given all over the world, do not cover topics that test or predict the skills to be used once students are admitted to a university. In this new millennium of computer technology, global communication, and the great variety of choices available to students of higher learning, it should be possible to devise new ways of selecting students and providing opportunities.

EXAMINING THE PERSUASION ESSAY

To persuade means to convince someone that you have good reasons for your opinion on a controversial topic. Your reader may or may not agree with your opinion, but the purpose of your **persuasion essay** is to provide strong examples to show that your reasons are real and true.

The topic of mandatory tests for university entrance brings out strong reaction in this essay with the thesis statement: *Not only are traditional university entrance exams impractical and ineffective, but also they cause undue amounts of stress on the test-takers. Accordingly, such tests should be abolished.* Notice that, as seen here, a thesis statement can be written in more than one sentence. The body of this sample essay supports this opinion.

 ## Your Turn!

Answer the following questions about *Arguments against Entrance Exams* in order to understand the **persuasion essay** and how it is constructed.

1. What are two examples from the first body paragraph that support the idea that these exams are impractical?
2. What are two examples from the next paragraph that support the opinion that these tests are not effective predictors of a student's success in school?
3. What are two examples of stress caused by these exams?

WRITE!

When you are deciding on a good topic for a **persuasion essay,** you need to begin with a controversial topic. You must be sure that you can provide factual evidence for support of your opinion, and you must be careful not to base your opinion on emotional reactions to the topic.

Look at another **persuasion essay** on page 167! Then try writing one yourself!

If you're having trouble thinking of a topic, here are some ideas for a **persuasion essay.**

- mandatory military service
- taking classes without grades (just pass/fail)
- one language for the whole world
- living and working in a foreign country
- required voting in all elections
- living together before marriage

Checklist for a Persuasion Essay

CONTENT

GOOD OK NEEDS WORK

____ ____ ____ The essay states an opinion for a topic that usually evokes strong opinions.

____ ____ ____ The essay provides clear, logical arguments for the stated opinion.

____ ____ ____ The essay relies on concrete examples rather than on emotion.

____ ____ ____ The essay forcefully states an opinion.

____ ____ ____ The essay uses "word pictures" to show the examples.

ORGANIZATION

GOOD OK NEEDS WORK

____ ____ ____ The introductory paragraph acknowledges that the topic can bring out an opinion quite contrary to the one in this essay.

____ ____ ____ The thesis statement clearly states the opinion to be expressed in this essay.

____ ____ ____ Each paragraph of the body begins with a topic sentence.

____ ____ ____ Each of the body paragraphs provides clear reasons for the stated opinion.

____ ____ ____ The body paragraphs connect to each other with transition words or phrases.

____ ____ ____ The concluding paragraph restates the thesis and gives a summary of the essay's arguments.

MECHANICS

YES   NO

____ ____ Does each sentence have a subject, a verb, and a complete thought?

____ ____ Does each sentence begin with a capital letter and end with a period?

____ ____ Do all the word combinations (subject-verb, adjective-noun, noun-pronoun) agree with each other?

____ ____ Does the verb tense express the appropriate time in each sentence?

____ ____ Are all the words spelled correctly?

____ ____ Are the articles (a, an, the) used correctly?

____ ____ Are the forms of the words (verb, noun, adjective) used correctly?

____ ____ Are all the word choices appropriate?

____ ____ Are all the sentences in correct order?

Got It!
The Overuse of Pronouns

Pronouns are the words that writers use to replace specific nouns. The problem is that when writers use too many pronouns in their writing, they can completely confuse their readers. To show you what we mean, try reading the paragraph about university entrance exams and see if you can understand the intended meaning for each *them, they, his or her, those, others,* and *it* without reading each sentence several times.

Scores on them do not effectively predict his or her performance. Some of them, who despite poor performance on class homework or presentations, or with poor attendance, can still perform well on the multiple-choice items. Others of them, despite their natural intelligence and high IQ's, are lazy, uninterested, and disruptive in the classroom. Still others who perform extremely well in class are prone to do well on them rather than on multiple-choice exams. For any of them, it will be unable to predict their performance once they reach a university. Furthermore, academic achievement in the areas tested does not ensure social and psychological adaptation to university life and work. It seems strange that they, often expensive and prestigious, would base their decision of admission so greatly on it when the test cannot distinguish between those who would contribute to it and those who would merely feed off it.

Rewrite the paragraph above replacing some (not all) of the pronouns with other nouns or proper nouns so that it is easier to understand. Use the space provided below.

_____

_____

_____

_____

_____

_____

_____

_____

_____

_____

_____

_____

_____

_____

_____

_____

_____

_____

_____

_____

_____

_____

_____

_____

_____

_____

Look at the following sample corrected paragraph. Did you make similar choices in pronouns and noun usage in your rewrite? What did you do differently? Why?

Scores on these languages and mathematics exams do not effectively predict student performance in the university. There are some students, who despite poor performance on class homework and presentations, or with poor attendance, can still perform well on multiple-choice items. Some students, despite their natural intelligence and high IQ's, are lazy, uninterested, and disruptive in the classroom. Still other students who perform extremely well in class are prone to do well on essay-style exams rather than on multiple-choice tests. For many of these students, an entrance exam will be unable to predict their performance once they reach a university. Furthermore, academic achievement in the areas tested does not ensure social and psychological adaptation to university life and work. It seems strange that institutions of higher learning, often expensive and in their own rights, prestigious, would base their decision of admissions so greatly on one test because the test cannot distinguish between students who would contribute to the school and those who would merely feed off the school.

Peer Feedback Form

The following is a list of more elements to examine when you read a classmate's writing or your own. The list can be used as a short peer feedback form, or it can be used with the main Peer Feedback Form on page 63.

(CIRCLE ONE)

1. **True** **False**   Each body paragraph has at least one example or detail to show that the topic sentence is true. The detail and/or example in each body paragraph is:

   Body Paragraph 1: _____

   Body Paragraph 2: _____

   Body Paragraph 3: _____

2. **True** **False**   In this essay, I found a word that was used in the wrong form. (For example, the noun ***difference*** should have been in the adjective form ***different***.)

   Wrong Form: _____

   Correction: _____

3. **True** **False**   The writer misuses articles *(a, an, the)* in the essay.

   Mistake: _____

   Correction: _____

4.7 The Definition Essay

WHAT DOES IT DO?

- A **definition essay** clearly shows what an idea or a word means.
- It clearly shows, with details and/or examples, the situations in which the idea or word has different meanings.
- It may discuss the origin of a word, especially if there is more than one meaning.

WHAT DOES IT CONTAIN?

- A **definition essay** has a clear thesis statement that indicates what idea/word is going to be defined. The thesis statement also tells the reader whether or not the definition changes according to situation.
- Each body paragraph discusses a situation in which the word/idea has a particular meaning, the people to whom the word/idea has a specific meaning, and/or the era in which the word/idea had a specific meaning.
- This essay concludes with a restatement of the thesis and a summary of the situations/definitions from the body paragraphs.

WHAT DOES IT DISCUSS?

The **definition essay** sometimes talks about new words/concepts. This essay may discuss how a definition has changed over time. Another possible topic is how the word/idea has different meanings for different groups of people or different meanings in different settings. This essay is usually written in the present tense, but if it talks about definitions over time, the simple past or present perfect tenses are used.

The Many Meanings of Date

When did you have your first date? Was it a bicycle ride with a girl or boy in elementary school? Was it a dinner and a movie in college? The word *date,* both a noun and a verb, has a variety of meanings in American English. Depending on one's sex, age, and family culture, *date* can have a different meaning for each person.

Gender plays an important part in determining how this one English word will be used. You may have heard women talking about going out on "dates" with their girlfriends, but rarely do you hear men use *date* to refer to get-togethers with friends of the same sex. Women use *date* in more than one way: in reference to their friends, as mentioned above, and also when talking about romantic meetings between one man and one woman. A get-together between groups of men and women or between two or more couples is also called "date" by women. Men, on the other hand, have a very specific usage for the word *date.* They use it only in reference to a planned event with one possible romantic partner.

The difference in semantics also changes with age. A common modern generational gap has to do with the way young people and older people define a *date.* Grandmothers and grandfathers from their mid-seventies and older may define a *date* as a young man and a woman having a cup of coffee or a walk in the park. And many old people would never think a couple could date without first meeting each other's parent. To the complete contrary, today's young adults would rarely think of introducing themselves to the parents of a *date* partner. The younger generation sees a *date* as a casual meeting or a short-term interlude whereas older people view the *date* as an important part of the courtship, a process that must ultimately lead to marriage.

Besides age and gender, one's family setting has a great impact on how one defines *date*. In a conservative household, the concept of dating may not even be relevant to girls or boys under the age of eighteen while in more open family settings, a broader definition may be given to dating. Consequently, dating would be a natural occurrence even at ages as young as five or six. In single-parent families, dating is for the single parent, mother or father, as well as for the kids once they reach an age the parent feels is appropriate. In this setting, a *date* may be an informal, common point of interest for older child and parent. In a two-parent family or in an extended family, dating would only be for the older children and as such, would have rules and guidelines surrounding it. The family religion or ethnicity may forbid dating until a certain age, and even then place restrictions on the types of *dates* regarding location of the date, religion of the other person, clothing to be worn on the *date,* and other possible limitations. The family plays a strong role in forming its youngest members' definition of *date*.

Despite the fact that the dictionary has very clear meanings for the word *date*, individuals form their own meanings, nuances, and usages for the word based on their gender, age, and family background. The next time someone asks you for a *date,* will it be a man or a woman, your friend, or your spouse? Will you accept or decline the invitation? The answers depend solely on your own personal meaning of *date*.

EXAMINING THE DEFINITION ESSAY

The **definition essay** takes a word or a concept that can be described or explained from a number of angles. Most frequently, definitions of a word or a concept vary depending on different circumstances.

This sample essay begins with the word to be defined and proceeds to this thesis statement: *Depending on one's sex, age, and family culture,* **date** *can have a different meaning for each person.* Each of these meanings is made clear in the body paragraphs.

 Your Turn!

Answer the following questions about *The Many Meanings of* Date in order to understand the **definition essay** and how it is constructed.

1. What is the biggest difference between men and women when they use the word *date*?
2. What is a generational difference in the definition of *date*?
3. What is a *date* for each of the following groups?
   a. a conservative family
   b. a single-parent family
   c. an extended family

WRITE!

Topics for **definition essays** do not come from a dictionary, but from different situations for the same word or concept. Your definition can come from groups of people in different situations, or it can come from the same person depending on his or her mood at the time that he or she creates the definition.

Can you think of a word or concept that you are familiar with? How many different definitions does it have? What do those definitions depend on? Before you write, take a look at the definition essay on page 171!

If you're having trouble thinking of a topic, here are some ideas for a **definition essay.**

- a good friend
- a perfect dating partner or mate
- being in style

- the worst/best job for me
- an effective leader
- the biggest problem in my country

Checklist for a Definition Essay

CONTENT

GOOD OK NEEDS WORK

____ ____ ____ The essay clarifies the meaning of a word or concept.

____ ____ ____ The essay shows that this word or concept is subject to different interpretations depending on different situations.

____ ____ ____ The essay clearly illustrates the interpretation of the word or concept in these different situations.

____ ____ ____ The essay uses "word" pictures to show the meanings of the word or concept in different situations.

ORGANIZATION

GOOD OK NEEDS WORK

____ ____ ____ The introductory paragraph leads to a thesis statement.

____ ____ ____ The thesis statement declares what word or concept the essay will define.

____ ____ ____ Each paragraph in the body begins with a topic sentence.

____ ____ ____ Each body paragraph gives examples that show the meaning of the word or concept in different situations.

____ ____ ____ The body paragraphs connect to each other with transition words or phrases.

____ ____ ____ The concluding paragraph restates the thesis and summarizes the fact that the definition of the word or concept can vary according to different situations.

MECHANICS

YES NO

____ ____ Does each sentence have a subject, a verb, and a complete thought?

____ ____ Does each sentence begin with a capital letter and end with a period?

____ ____ Do all the word combinations (subject-verb, adjective-noun, noun-pronoun) agree with each other?

____ ____ Does the verb tense express the appropriate time in each sentence?

____ ____ Are all the words spelled correctly?

____ ____ Are the articles (a, an, the) used correctly?

____ ____ Are the forms of the words (verb, noun, adjective) used correctly?

____ ____ Are all the word choices appropriate?

____ ____ Are all the sentences in correct order?

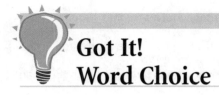

Got It!
Word Choice

The word *date* is both a noun and a verb and has different meanings depending on the way it is used, as you learned in the model definition essay. There are also shades of meaning (nuances) that determine different uses for the synonyms of an adjective. For example, there are several adjectives listed as synonyms for the word *little*: *small, tiny, petite,* and *insignificant.* However, there are big differences in the actual uses of these words. They cannot all be used interchangeably. For example: a baby (male or female) might be very *small* or *tiny.* A grown woman might be *petite* or *tiny,* but a grown man would be insulted to be described as *tiny* or as *petite.* Furthermore, a human of any age would resent being labeled *insignificant* (meaning: of very small importance). When you are writing your essays, you want to be sure that your word choices are precise. Therefore, it is a good idea to consult a dictionary with clear examples that illustrate these nuances or shades of meaning.

   a. Here are three adjective synonyms that appear to have the same meaning, but they are actually used in very different descriptive situations.

   large   **enormous**   **vast**

   Write a sentence that illustrates the appropriate usage for each of the above adjectives in a specific descriptive situation.

   1._____

   2._____

   3._____

   b. Another problem of word choice involves the word ***thing***. Many beginning writers have difficulty finding words to name ideas or other inanimate objects, so they overuse the word ***thing***. Look at the following paragraph.

   There are three things that make a good friendship. The first thing is honesty. Friendship is too important a thing to be damaged by lies and rumors. If a friend cannot be trusted, there is no difference between that person and a stranger. Another thing is common interest. If two people are interested in the same things, it is easier for them to have conversations through which they can get closer to one another. The third and most important thing is respect. Friends need to understand what things bother each other or make the other person sad. Then it is each friend's job to be sensitive to those things. Honesty, commonality, and respect are things that create lasting friendships.

Wow! This paragraph used the word *thing(s)* nine times! There are a variety of other words that can be used in place of *thing*. Look at the words below. Then rewrite the above paragraph replacing *thing(s)* at least six of the nine times. Although the nouns are synonyms, they also have differing uses, so look them up in a dictionary before you put them in your paragraph. Write your new paragraph in the space provided.

concept	unit	part
characteristic	aspect	kind
element	factor	issue
idea	matter	concern

_____

_____

_____

_____

_____

_____

_____

_____

Peer Feedback Form

The following is a list of more elements to examine when you read a classmate's writing or your own. The list can be used as a short peer feedback form, or it can be used with the main Peer Feedback Form on page 63.

(CIRCLE ONE)

1. **True False**   The writer does not overuse pronouns. It is clear to whom or what the pronouns refer.

                       If false, give an example of a sentence with (an) unclear pronoun(s).

                       _____

                       _____

1. **True False**   The author clearly uses first person, second person, or third person.*

                       ***It is confusing to the reader when the author uses some sentences in the first person (I), other sentences in the third person (she), and still others in the second person (you). The position from which the writer composes must remain consistent throughout the entire essay.**

1. **True False**   There are clear words or phrases that indicate the conclusion of the essay. One word or phrase is: _____.

Mechanics Review

5.1 Sentence Fragments and Run-on Sentences

A **sentence fragment** is only a part of a sentence. It is not a complete thought even though it may have both a subject and a verb.

A **run-on** is a combination of two or more complete sentences that are incorrectly punctuated as one sentence.

Here is one paragraph from a **narrative essay** in this book. The paragraph below does not have punctuation or capitalization to show complete sentences. Correct this paragraph so that it has complete sentences with capital letters, periods, and commas. Don't peek at the original essay!

. . . . then it was off to the grocery store to pick up the cake that added more stress we picked up the cake and saw blonde bride and groom plastic figurines on the top these blondes did not resemble my Korean fiancé or my Italian self we took the cake to the restaurant where the reception was to be held the next day following the wedding as I took it out of the car the cake fell against the side of its box consequently I had two blonde figurines standing on a

dented wedding cake the owner of the restaurant and I set the cake strategically on a table in the corner the dented side was against a wall then I got out
a marker and started coloring the figurines' heads as luck would have it the
marker ran out of ink the bride had a full head of new black hair and the groom
had a head of two colors I was tired tomorrow was my wedding day those figurines would provide entertainment I decided mistakenly thinking tomorrow
would be a better day.

subordinate because it starts with as

SPECIAL SENTENCE FRAGMENT PROBLEMS

Words like **because, so,** and **but** are often used as connectors between clauses. A
clause is a group of related words with a subject and a verb. An independent
clause is a full sentence with a clear meaning. A dependent clause is not a full sentence and cannot be used alone. It needs more information to be clear.

The following are punctuated as sentences, but they are not complete sentences
because they are only part of a thought.

1. Because he was sick.
2. So we drove to the beach.
3. But my mother wanted to stay at home.

Your Turn!

We need to add a clause (another idea) to each of these dependent clauses in
order to form complete sentences.

1. Because he was sick.

   Examples: **My teacher stayed home last week because he was sick.**

   or

   John missed the test again because he was sick.

   or

   My brother told me that he couldn't go to the opera because he was sick.

   Your sentence: ___He didn't come to the___ because he was sick.
                                      game

2. So we drove to the beach.

   Example: **The weather was beautiful, so we drove to the beach.**

   Your sentence: ___My kids came___, so we drove to the beach.
                       out of school early.

3. But my mother wanted to stay at home.

   Example: **My father wanted to go out to eat, but my mother wanted to stay at home.**

   Your sentence: ___I wanted to vist my___, but my mother
                      wanted to stay at home.   couson

4. *Now write three more completely different sentences using each of the connectors.*

   because: ___I couldn't wake up becaus I stade___
                up late

   but: ___I _____ police car

   so: ___I was early, so I went to the library___

MORE PRACTICE WITH FRAGMENTS

The following word groups are also **sentence fragments**. Add words to these fragments so that they become complete thoughts and complete sentences.

Example: Because my brother has not finished high school yet

Because my brother has not finished high school yet, my family has decided not to move.

Your Turn!

1. while I watched that horror movie with my younger sister, I was feeling asleep.

2. because David wanted to meet a woman who had recently traveled in Africa, made an apoinment to see her.

3. but the clock ran out and our team lost the championship game
   we were losing by one point, but the colck

4. so we realized we were in trouble and we had to think of a clever solution
   We came late, so we realized we were

5. although he was not the man of her dreams, not rich, not handsome, not even the slightest bit interesting or exciting, she married him.

PRACTICE WITH RUN-ON SENTENCES

The following word groups are **run-on sentences.** We can correct each of these sentences by adding appropriate conjunctions to connect the thoughts or by breaking them into separate sentences.

Example: **Last summer my family drove from California to New York we had many amusing experiences.**

Last summer my family drove from California to New York, *and* we had many amusing experiences.

or

Last summer *when* my family drove from California to New York, we had many amusing experiences.

or

Last summer my family drove from California to New York. *We* had many amusing experiences.

 # Your Turn!

Correct the following run-on sentences and rewrite them in the space provided.

1. Slowly she opened the door then the mouse ran across her foot and her scream pierced the air.

   _____

   _____

2. The judge declared the man guilty he had stolen a pig from a farmer who had planned to use that pig to feed his very hungry family of twelve children.

    _____

    _____

3. We watched a hilarious comedy at the newest theater downtown after that we drove to an Italian restaurant for pizza, spaghetti, and lasagna finally we told each other goodnight and went home.

    _____

    _____

4. The woman was an entertaining clown she was also a serious actress.

    _____

    _____

5. Stop complaining be optimistic.

    _____

    _____

5.2 Subject-Verb Agreement

The subject and the verb must agree. If the subject of a sentence or a clause is singular, its verb must be in the same form. In the same way, plural subjects require plural verbs.

The following are some sentences from a process essay in this book. Find the subjects and choose the correct verb forms. Don't peek at the essay!

1. The easiest place to look for homes (**is/are**) in the newspaper's classified section.

2. If the city or area (**is/are**) large, the ads will be listed according to neighborhood.

3. (**Is/Are**) there water stains or chipped paint?

4. It is usually a one or two-page document that (**lists/list**) all the rules you and the owner (**has to/have to**) follow.

5. Most (**is/are**) one-year leases, but there (**is/are**) also six-month leases.

 Your Turn!

Now see if you can find the subjects of the following sentences and then choose the verbs that agree with them.

1. One of the main reasons John decided to study Spanish (**was/were**) because he (**lives/live**) near the Mexican border.

2. Some people who (**has/have**) a house in Hawaii (**does/do**) not know very much about the natives who unfortunately (**is/are**) slowly vanishing.

3. Nearly every member of my high school graduating class (**has/have**) been accepted to one of the universities that (**is/are**) rated as excellent.

4. On the concrete floor of the garage (**was/were**) a pile of ashes from the fire that (**was/were**) started by some young boys who (**was/were**) playing with matches.

5. Some of the most popular actors in India (**appears/appear**) in a different movie every few weeks because India (**makes/make**) more movies than any other country.

5.3 Verb Tenses

Verb tenses are used to clarify the "time" in an essay. Various forms of the present tense are used in most essays, but the narrative essay is a type of writing that often uses a combination of tenses. For example, while writers mostly relate events from the past in their narrative essays, they also sometimes refer to their present feelings about these events.

The following sentences are taken from a narrative essay in which different times and, therefore, different verb tenses should be used. Look for time clues to help you decide which tenses are appropriate. Then write in the verb tense that makes the time of the sentence clear.

1. Before my trip to Portugal, I had always _____ (travel) with a group, so someone else _____ (plan) and _____ (carry out) all my travel arrangements. Therefore, I _____ (look) forward to what I _____ (think) _____ (be) an adventure.

2. A thief _____ (steal) my purse, so trips to the credit card, travelers' check, and airline offices further _____ (consume) the time that we _____ (intend) to spend at Faro, a beach resort.

3. Today I still _____ (regret) the experience, but it _____ (not change) my impression of Lisbon. It _____ (be) still one of the most beautiful places I _____ (ever see).

Your Turn!

Now see if you can choose correct verb tenses for these sentences.

1. I _____ (hold) my breath in fear when I _____ (discover) that I accidentally _____ (step on) the foot of a huge, angry man.

2. Last summer, while I _____ (swim) off the coast of Australia, the thought of sharks sometimes _____ (frighten) me and I _____ (wish) I _____ (go) to a swimming pool instead.

3. After that day, I _____ (know) that Jake _____ (never marry) me, and I _____ (promise) myself never to fall in love with another man as long as I _____ (live).

4. Then I _____ (realize) if I _____ (tell) my father the truth, he _____ (give) me another chance. From that day until this one, I _____ (never lie) again.

5. Two weeks ago, the guests _____ (wait) in the church, and the organist _____ (play) the Wedding March when my brother and his fiancée _____ (come) down the aisle together and _____ (announce) that they _____ (change) their minds. There _____ (be) no wedding after all.

5.4 Articles

The use of the articles **a, an,** and **the** can cause problems in sentence writing. These are general rules for their usage.

Singular Count Noun Rules
1. **If the noun is only one of a larger group, use *a* or *an*.**
   Examples: He is *a* student.
   I eat ***an*** apple every day.
2. **If the noun is a specific one of a larger group, use *the*.**
   Examples: He is ***the*** student with red hair. I eat ***the*** apple that is ***the*** ripest every day.

Plural Count Noun Rules
1. **If the nouns are specific, use *the*.**
   Example: They are ***the*** students with red hair. They eat ***the*** ripest apples.
2. **If they are not specific, do not use any article.**
   Example: They are students. They eat ripe apples.

Non-count Noun Rules
1. **If the noun is specific, use *the*.**
   Example: He likes to read about ***the*** life of actors.
2. **If the noun is general, do not use any article.**
   Example: He learned from his experience that life is not always fair.

Here are some sentences from one of the essays in this book. Fill in the blank with the article that best completes the sentence. Your choices are: **a, an, the, X** (X = no article). Don't peek!

Once you have decided, you will need to sign _____ lease. _____ lease is _____ agreement between you and _____ owner. It is usually _____ one- or two-page document that lists all _____ rules both you and _____ owner have to follow. It will include information about _____ rent, _____ deposit, pets, utility payments, deposits for _____ damages, and most importantly, _____ length of _____ time that you can live in _____ place.

Your Turn!

Now you try it: Make sentences for the following.

an answer

_____

the answer

_____

doctors

_____

the doctors

_____

education

_____

the education

_____

5.5 Adjectives: Active or Passive?

When adjectives are formed from verbs, they can be active (present participle form) or passive (past participle form). The adjective is active *(-ing)* when the noun that it modifies performs an action. The adjective is passive *(-ed)* when the noun that it modifies receives the action.

Look at the difference in meaning in the active and passive adjectives of these sentences:

> The **boring** professor (the professor is boring the students) told the **bored** class (the students are bored by the professor) the same old jokes at every class meeting.
>
> The **interested** young man can't wait to learn more about the **interesting** young woman he met at a party.
>
> The **fascinating** lecture about the strange insects of Africa kept the audience **fascinated** for two hours.
>
> "The slow, scary climb up the first loop is the most **exciting** part!" shouted my **excited** cousin as she raced to get in line for a second ride on the roller coaster.

Here are some sentences from one of the cause and effect essays in this book. Fill in the correct active or passive adjective forms for each sentence.

An American foreign exchange student _____ Portuguese in
  studying/studied
Brazil was having a weekly lesson with his Brazilian teacher. The teacher had

just finished a long, _____ explanation of a grammar point, so
         complicating/complicated
she asked her student if he understood what she had just said . . . The

American was _____ . . . Body language, and particularly
       bewildering/bewildered
gestures, can be just as different from country to country as _____
                     speaking/spoken
languages, and more particularly, just as important.

Your Turn!

Make sentences using both the active and the passive forms of these adjectives. Be sure you use them to describe nouns. Do not use them as verbs.

ACTIVE	PASSIVE
writing	written
burning	burned/burnt
challenging	challenged

Write a sentence with **writing** as an adjective:

_____

Write a sentence with **written** as an adjective:

_____

Write a sentence with **burning** as an adjective:

_____

Write a sentence with **burned/burnt** as an adjective:

_____

Write a sentence with **challenging** as an adjective:

_____

Write a sentence with **challenged** as an adjective:

_____

5.6 Word Forms: Verb, Noun, or Adjective?

Sometimes the meaning of a word is perfectly clear, but its form should be changed according to its grammatical use in a sentence. Three forms that are often confused with each other are the verb form, the noun form, and the adjective form.

> *If the word is used to show an action or make a statement,*
> *the word needs to be in its **verb form**.*
>   **Example:** Soccer and football **differ** in some important ways.

> *If the word is used as a name, it needs to be in its **noun form**.*
>   **Example:** One big **difference** is in the shape of the ball used in football
>   and in soccer.

> *If the word modifies a noun, it needs to be in its **adjective form**.*
>   **Example:** There are **different** rules regarding the use of the hands in
>   football and in soccer.

If you are not sure which form is correct, first decide how the word is used in the sentence (action/statement, name, or description). Sometimes you can rewrite a sentence to be sure that you are using the correct form. For example, in a comparison/contrast essay in this book, this sentence appears:

> Furthermore, they (tour guides) may need to preview many places to
> **familiarize** (<u>verb</u>) themselves with museums and other sites.

The sentence could be restructured in this way: . . . they may need to become **familiar** (<u>adjective</u>) with museums and other sites . . . or . . . they may need to develop a **familiarity** (<u>noun</u>) with museums and other sites . . .

> *Another sentence from this essay states:*
> This student-teaching setting is where prospective teachers first learn
> of the **importance** (<u>noun</u>) of specific lesson **preparation** (<u>noun</u>).

The sentence could be restructured in this way: The student-teaching or practice setting is where prospective teachers first learn that it is **important** (<u>adjective</u>) that they **prepare** (<u>verb</u>) for specific lessons.

Your Turn!

Make sentences with these words in each of these forms:

VERBS	**NOUNS**	**ADJECTIVES**
compare	comparison	comparative
beautify	beauty	beautiful
observe	observation	observant

Write a sentence with **compare:**

_____

Write a sentence with **comparison:**

_____

Write a sentence with **comparative:**

_____

Write a sentence with **beautify:**

_____

Write a sentence with **beauty:**

_____

Write a sentence with **beautiful:**

_____

Write a sentence with **observe:**

_____

Write a sentence with **observation:**

_____

Write a sentence with **observant:**

_____

Sample Student Essays

The essays in this section were written by ESL writers in a preparation class for community college entrance. For each essay, there is a **rough draft,** a **checklist** of corrections that students needed to make, and a **revised draft** of the essay. The rough drafts include errors. These essays were chosen because they demonstrate the extent to which students, all using the same basic rules of the multiparagraph format, are able to self-check; implement corrections; and at the same time, show some degree of personal style and character. You will notice this in the fact that the essays differ not only in topic, but also in length and detail.

6.1 Student Narrative Essay

ROUGH DRAFT

Scare of Fireworks

Normally, we used to play fireworks even just looking. It is so excite and funny game. On the other hand, it can be danger game even though we don't care about it. By the way, when I was twelve years old, I started to play fireworks with my friends. Fireworks have been popular game around my ages in that time

First, I played skyrockets with my friends in the park nobody used, just like opening. We always played to throw them at each other. One day we went off throwing them at each other. Then we threw sky rockets to some house. We were kind of silly we didn't know what happen as we know now. Many police cars came and shouted, "what the hell are you doing, boys!" I had never seen many police cars before. We had experienced to be chased; however. It was just one or two cars, but we saw six cars in that time. We suddenly went away from that place. We rode our bicycles. The police had six cars and called other policemen with bicycles. We thought we could escape this situation if they had just six cars because it had many narrow roads that cars can't go through, but they called many (about 10–15) policemen with bicycles we had to ride our bicycles faster as much as possible. Somehow, we ran away from them.

Then we went to school without thinking about yesterday. After school, homeroom teacher called our names to come to the reception room. We went to there then we surprised that most of teachers were there. Of course we had to be punished for two or three hours long by many teachers.

After that, the policemen came to ask us about that for two or three hours. They took notes and watched us. I felt I wanted to weep. Then the policemen scolded us for awhile, after that, we could go back to home.

However, I didn't want to go to home because my teacher called my parents about that. I thought my parents would shout at me all night. Anyway, I had to go back and naturally my parents did it. I got some punches from my father, then I went into fits, so I didn't get punish all night. I woke up and went to school next day. I saw everybody had something like scars by parents or someone punished them. I also had a scar around my eye.

You can play fireworks even though you can control yourself and be safe. If not, you must not do. I think I learned something good from this experience.

Student-Completed Checklist
for a Narrative Essay

CONTENT

GOOD   OK   NEEDS WORK

GOOD	OK	NEEDS WORK	
____	✓	____	The essay clearly expresses the writer's feelings about an event.
✓	____	____	The essay includes the time and place of this event.
✓	____	____	The essay makes clear which other people played a part in this event.
____	✓	____	The essay uses "word pictures" to show the event.

ORGANIZATION

GOOD   OK   NEEDS WORK

GOOD	OK	NEEDS WORK	
____	____	✓	The introductory paragraph leads to a thesis statement.
____	____	✓	The thesis statement declares the event and the writer's feeling.
____	✓	____	Each paragraph in the body has a topic sentence.
✓	____	____	The body paragraphs follow a chronological order.
____	✓	____	The body paragraphs connect to each other with transition words or phrases.
____	✓	____	The essay builds to a high point or climax.
____	____	✓	The concluding paragraph restates the thesis and summarizes the narrative.

MECHANICS

YES	NO	
✓	____	Does each sentence have a subject, a verb, and a complete thought?
____	✓	Does each sentence begin with a capital letter and end with a period?
✓	____	Do all the word combinations (subject-verb, adjective-noun, noun-pronoun) agree with each other?
____	✓	Does the verb tense express the appropriate time in each sentence?
✓	____	Are all the words spelled correctly?
____	✓	Are the articles (*a, an, the*) used correctly?
____	✓	Are the forms of the words (verb, noun, adjective) used correctly?
✓	____	Are all the word choices appropriate?
____	✓	Are all the sentences in correct order?

REVISED DRAFT
The Scare of Fireworks

When I was twelve years old, I started to play with fireworks with my friends. Normally, we used to play fireworks just by watching them. It was such an exciting and funny game. On the other hand, it could be a dangerous game.

First, I played with fireworks with my friends in the park where there was an open space. We always played by throwing them at each other. Then we threw skyrockets at some houses near the park. We were kind of silly and we didn't know what would happen next. Many police cars came and the policemen shouted, "What the hell are you doing, boys?" I had never seen as many police cars before. We had experienced being chased; however, it was just one or two cars, but we saw six cars at that time.

We suddenly went away from that place. We rode our bicycles. The police had six cars and called other policemen with bicycles. We thought we could escape this situation if they had just six cars because there were many roads that cars couldn't go through, but they called about ten to fifteen policemen with bicycles. We had to ride our bicycles as fast as possible. Somehow, we got away from them.

Then we went to school the next day without thinking about yesterday. After school, the homeroom teacher called our names to come to the reception room. We went there and were surprised that most of the teachers were there. Of course, we had to be punished for two or three hours long by ten to fifteen teachers, but we were just six people. After that, the policemen came to ask us about the incident for two or three hours. They took notes and watched us. I felt like I wanted to weep. Then the policemen scolded us for a while, and after that, we could go back home.

However, I didn't want to go home because my teacher called my parents about the incident. I thought my parents would shout at me all night. Anyway, I had to go back and my parents did shout at me. I got some punches from my father and then I went into fits, so I didn't get punished all night.

I woke up and went to school the next day. I saw everybody that was with me had something like scars from parents or someone who punished them. I also had a scar around my eye.

I think I learned something good from this experience. You can play with fireworks if you can control yourself and be safe. If not, you must not do it.

6.2 Student Process Essay

ROUGH DRAFT
Derisious and Easy

What is your favorite food? If someone questioned me about what is my favorite food, I can answer right away that my favorite food is curry & rice. I often cook curry & rice because it is very easy to cook and we can cook many kinds of curry and rice depend on our idea.

The first thing to do is buy the ingredients for the curry & rice. We can buy all of ingredients for the curry & rice in a grocery store. For common curry & rice with potatos, onions, carrots, some meat and of course curry powder. There are some kinds of curry powder in a grocery store, very spicy, avarge, hot taste, not quite spicy, so you can chose curry powder. Also it's good idea to mix curry powder.

After you arrive home, you need to cut all ingredients likely size for the curry. When you cut all ingredients, you need to think of the time you have because potatos and carrots are spent long time to cook so if you cut these big size you have to spend very long time to cook. After you cut all ingredients, preheating the pot and put little oil into the pot and fry with spatula for 1 or 2 minuits then put potatos and carrots into the pot and fry for 1 or 2 minuits then put onions and some water into the pot. We need water about covering ingredients. After that shut the pot and give it a good boil.

Usually, it takes 30 minuits. If it spend 30 minuits you need check it that the ingredients cooked well done or not. If it is enough, put curry powder into the pot then mix it and simmer it about 5 minuits. After that serve curry with rice in a dish and eat!

You can make derisious curry few ingredients. It's very conveinent and easy. Also curry scent is make our mouth water. Moreover you can make your own curry by your idea. Is there better food than curry? I think there is no better food than curry.

Student-Completed Checklist for a Process Essay

CONTENT

GOOD	OK	NEEDS WORK	
------	----	-----------	
✓	___	___	The essay thoroughly explains how to follow a process.
✓	___	___	The essay includes all the necessary steps to complete a process.
___	✓	___	The essay clearly shows how to complete each step of a process.
___	✓	___	The essay uses "word pictures" to show the process.

ORGANIZATION

GOOD	OK	NEEDS WORK	
------	----	-----------	
___	✓	___	The introductory paragraph leads to a thesis statement.
___	✓	___	The thesis statement clearly declares what process is to be explained.
___	✓	___	Each paragraph in the body begins with a topic sentence.
✓	___	___	The body paragraphs follow a logical order to show completion of the process.
___	___	✓	The body paragraphs connect to each other with transition words or phrases.
___	✓	___	The concluding paragraph restates the thesis and summarizes the process.

MECHANICS

YES	NO	
-----	----	
___	✓	Does each sentence have a subject, a verb, and a complete thought?
___	✓	Does each sentence begin with a capital letter and end with a period?
✓	___	Do all the word combinations (subject-verb, adjective-noun, noun-pronoun) agree with each other?
✓	___	Does the verb tense express the appropriate time in each sentence?
___	✓	Are all the words spelled correctly?
___	✓	Are the articles (*a, an, the*) used correctly?
___	✓	Are the forms of the words (verb, noun, adjective) used correctly?
___	✓	Are all the word choices appropriate?
___	✓	Are all the sentences in correct order?

REVISED DRAFT
Delicious and Easy

What is your favorite food? If someone questioned me about what my favorite food is, I can answer right away that my favorite food is curry and rice. I often cook curry and rice because it is very easy to cook and because, depending on different ideas, there are many kinds of curry and rice.

To cook curry and rice, the first thing to do is to buy the ingredients. You can buy all of the ingredients for curry and rice in any grocery store. For common curry and rice, you will need potatoes, onions, carrots, some beef or chicken for meat, and of course, curry powder. There are some different kinds of curry powder, for example, very spicy, medium hot taste, and not quite spicy, so you can choose your favorite curry powder. You could also mix different curry powders with each other for an unusual taste.

After you get home from the grocery store, it is time to begin the preparation of your curry and rice. First, you need to cut all the ingredients into a likely size for the curry. When you do the cutting, you need to think about how much time you have for cooking. Potatoes and carrots take a long time to cook, so if you cut them into large pieces, you will spend a very long time cooking. After you cut up all the ingredients, preheat a pot. Put a little oil into the pot and spread the oil by moving the pot so that the bottom of it is covered with oil. Next, put the chicken or beef in the pot and fry it with a spatula for one or two minutes. Put the potatoes and carrots in and continue to fry for one or two minutes more. Now add the onions and some water to the pot. You will need enough water to cover the ingredients. Finally, cover the pot and give it a good boil, usually for thirty minutes.

After the vegetables and meat have boiled for thirty minutes, you need to check to see if they are cooked well done or not. If they are cooked enough, add the curry powder to the pot. Stir it in to mix it well, and let the pot simmer for about five minutes more. When it is ready to eat, serve it in a bowl with rice.

You can make delicious and different curry and rice with only a few ingredients. It is also convenient and easy to prepare. In addition, the curry scent will make your mouth water! Use your own ideas to make your own special curry. I think you will agree with me that there is no better food than curry and rice.

6.3 Student Classification Essay

ROUGH DRAFT
Cultural Difficulties

I had just 1 year to finish my high school. In the summer time my parents let me to go to England for 2 months. Maybe I had a nice 2 months to practice my English. I have never my home country before. Of course, it would be my first chance. I didn't know that many cultural difficulties were waiting for me. When I was at the airport, it had already started.

That thing of course I was missing. You can be sure that it was my country. The first thing to do is I have to forget my home country. I never start to think about it. Because I was in different country I have to live there for a while. No chance to return back. If I want to think about my future I have to learn living in a different culture. I saw that restaurants, markets, people, traffic, population, everything are kind of different in other country. But I must try to new ones: Sometimes I like sometimes I don't but I have to live. For a while try to live like English. This helped me a lot. Now I am in England, I am saying to myself, "I am not Turkish, I transfer to English."

The second thing is who I am missing. Of course my parents and my friends. I had a lot of time with them in my home country. But now they were not close to me. Maybe I can talk to them only once a week. The thing that I have to do is searching for new friends. This was going to help me a lot. But make sure that the friend that I was searching must be from the country where I live. Then I'll forget that I was foreign person. It was very necessary for me. And they'll be very helpful for my living abroad.

Then what comes next? Of course, food. For food there was nothing to do if I can't find restaurants which makes my cultural food, it's quite bad for me. I must eat the other. But I think it is not impossible. I tried before. After 2 weeks I start to eat and I even start to like some of the food. I have to do this, but of course I rather eat food from my country.

In conclusion, there were, of course, a lot differences and difficulties in living abroad. If I choose to leave my country I have to change my living and also my mind. If I put it in my mind I can do it. I try to forget about what I used to do in my home country.

Student-Completed Checklist
for a Classification Essay

CONTENT

GOOD	OK	NEEDS WORK	
___	✓	___	The essay discusses a primary topic from which at least three subtopics can be formed.
___	✓	___	The essay explains each of the three subtopics and shows how they are related to the primary topic.
___	___	✓	The essay gives equal description or examples for each of the three subtopics.
___	___	✓	The essay uses "word pictures" to show the subtopics.

ORGANIZATION

GOOD	OK	NEEDS WORK	
___	___	✓	The introductory paragraph leads from a primary topic into at least three subtopics.
___	___	✓	The thesis statement states the subtopics and their relationship to the primary topic.
___	✓	___	Each body paragraph begins with a topic sentence.
___	✓	___	Each paragraph of the body clearly describes one of the three subtopics.
___	✓	___	The body paragraphs connect to each other with transition words or phrases.
___	✓	___	The concluding paragraph restates the thesis and brings the subtopics back to their primary topic.

MECHANICS

YES	NO	
___	✓	Does each sentence have a subject, a verb, and a complete thought?
___	✓	Does each sentence begin with a capital letter and end with a period?
✓	___	Do all the word combinations (subject-verb, adjective-noun, noun-pronoun) agree with each other?
___	✓	Does the verb tense express the appropriate time in each sentence?
✓	___	Are all the words spelled correctly?
___	✓	Are the articles (*a, an, the*) used correctly?
✓	___	Are the forms of the words (verb, noun, adjective) used correctly?
✓	___	Are all the word choices appropriate?
___	✓	Are all the sentences in correct order?

Cultural Difficulties

I had just one year to finish my high school. In the summer time my parents let me go to England for two months. I thought maybe I would have a nice two months to practice my English. I had never left my home country before. It would be my first chance. I didn't know that many cultural difficulties were waiting for me.

The biggest problem was that I missed my country. The first thing I had to do is forget my home country. I tried never to start to think about it because I was in a different country. I had to live there for a while with no chance to return home. If I wanted to think about my future, I had to learn to live in a different culture. I saw that restaurants, markets, people, traffic, size, everything was different in another country. I had to try new things. Sometimes I liked them and sometimes I didn't, but I had to live. For a while, I tried to live like the English, and this helped me a lot. Now, I was in England, so I said to myself, "I am not Turkish. I have transferred to English."

In addition to my country, I missed many people. Of course I missed my parents and my friends. I had a lot of time with them in my home country, but now they were not close to me. Maybe I could talk to them only once a week on the telephone or we sent e-mail to each other. The thing that I had to do was search for new friends. This was going to help me a lot, but I had to make sure that I was searching for friends from the country where I was living. Then I could forget that I was a foreign person. It was necessary for me, and they were very helpful for my living abroad. We had fun together and they helped me practice my English.

The last big cultural difficulty for me was food. At first I thought there was nothing to do if I couldn't find restaurants, which made my own cultural food. It would be very bad for me, and I might get sick because I would not have enough strength if I didn't eat as much as I usually did. However, it was not impossible to change. I tried other food, and after two weeks I started to eat it, and I even started to like some of the other food. I would still rather eat food from my own country, but my English friends showed me many different kinds of restaurants and most of them were not bad, and some of them were even very good.

In conclusion, I had some difficulties living in a different culture. However, I decided that if I chose to leave my country to go to another culture, I had to change my living and also my mind. If I put it in my mind, I could do it. I tried to forget about everything I used to do in my home country and to enjoy the new country.

6.4 Student Comparison/Contrast Essay

ROUGH DRAFT

Home Stay or Apartment

Which is prefer a home stay or an apartment when you live in the foreign country to study the foreign language? Some people choose an apartment because it is easy. With others, home stay is a lot of advantages to study the foreign language.

The first advantage is that if you choose a home stay which is included meals, you don't have to cook your meal. When you are busy with a lot of your assignment, and you might have no time to cook your meals. If you live in an apartment you might eat snacks, frozen food, or junk food, but it is not good for your health. On the other hand you live with your host family. They prepare your meals for you, so you can do your assignment.

The second advantage is that you speak the foreign language after you go back home. You come to the country to study the foreign language, so you had better talk to native people. If you have a home stay, you can talk about your school, friends and so on when you have dinner with your host family, and you can improve your foreign language.

The third advantage is that you have a lot of chance to meet other native people. Your host family's friends might come to their house and your host family introduce you, so you have chance to talk to them, and you might get along with them. If you go to a language school, or live in an apartment which every student is from other country, so it's difficult to get along with native people.

If you can find a good host family, you can spend a great time with them and you can learn the foreign culture, too. Those advantage make you happy.

Student-Completed Checklist
for a Comparison/Contrast Essay

CONTENT

GOOD	OK	NEEDS WORK	
✓	___	___	The essay compares and/or contrasts two related topics.
✓	___	___	The essay stresses either similarities or differences of its two topics.
___	✓	___	The essay provides equal details and examples for both topics.
___	___	✓	The essay uses "word pictures" to show the similarities/differences.

ORGANIZATION

GOOD	OK	NEEDS WORK	
___	✓	___	The introductory paragraph shows a basic relationship between the two topics and leads to a thesis statement.
___	___	✓	The thesis statement names both of the topics and states clearly whether the emphasis will be on the similarities or on the differences.
___	___	✓	Each body paragraph begins with a topic sentence.
✓	___	___	The essay shows corresponding differences or similarities of both topics in each of the body paragraphs.
___	___	✓	The essay uses transition words or phrases to connect the two topics.
___	___	✓	The essay concludes with a restatement of the thesis and reference to the differences or the similarities between the two topics.

MECHANICS

YES	NO	
___	✓	Does each sentence have a subject, a verb, and a complete thought?
✓	___	Does each sentence begin with a capital letter and end with a period?
___	✓	Do all the word combinations (subject-verb, adjective-noun, noun-pronoun) agree with each other?
___	✓	Does the verb tense express the appropriate time in each sentence?
✓	___	Are all the words spelled correctly?
___	✓	Are the articles (a, an, the) used correctly?
___	✓	Are the forms of the words (verb, noun, adjective) used correctly?
✓	___	Are all the word choices appropriate?
✓	___	Are all the sentences in correct order?

REVISED DRAFT

Home Stay or Apartment

Which is preferable, a home stay or an apartment when you live in a foreign country to study a foreign language? Some people choose an apartment just because they think it is easier, but maybe they should think about some of the advantages of living in a home stay. There are some important differences in living in an apartment or in a home stay when you study a foreign language. *main topic*

One big difference between living in an apartment or in a home stay is the food. When you are busy with a lot of your assignments, you might have no time to cook. If you live in an apartment, you might eat only snacks, frozen food, or junk, but they are not good for your health. If you choose a home stay that includes meals, you don't have to cook your own meals. They can prepare healthy meals for you with fresh fruits and vegetables. In addition, you don't have to use your time to buy the food at the supermarket or to cook it, so you have enough time to do all your homework.

Another difference is being able to practice the foreign language after school and on weekends. If you live alone in an apartment, there is no one to talk to for practice. If you have a roommate from your country, probably you will speak just your own language. You have come to the foreign country to study the language, so you had better talk to native people. If you have a home stay, you can talk about your school, friends, and other things when you have dinner with your host family. You can practice your conversation skills and learn many new idioms. Another good thing for the home stay is that you can ask questions if you don't understand something you hear on a television show or a movie that you watch in their house. The host family will help you to improve your speaking and your listening comprehension.

Another point of difference is the chance to meet many native people. If you live in an apartment building and only speak the foreign language to students from your language school, it is difficult to meet native people. A home stay is different because your host family's friends might come to their house and your host family introduces you. You have a chance to talk to them, and you might get along very well with them and become friends. When there is a holiday, you will probably meet more people in their family too, like grandparents, aunts, uncles and cousins. If you have a host family with kids, you will get to meet their friends when they come to the house. You can also talk to their neighbors if you want more practice.

There are important differences for foreign students in an apartment or in a home stay. If you can find a good host family, you can spend a great time with them, and you can practice the language. You can learn about the foreign culture, too. Those advantages will make you happy.

6.5 Student Cause and Effect Essay

Children Watching Television

Most people have TV and love TV show. It gives us a lot of informations, fun things, and sometimes sirious things. Especially children love to watch TV very much; however, watching television is bad for children.

There are a lot of violence TV programs. For example, in action TV programs, their favorite actors kill a lot of people easily. They are hero for children and children imitate their action to other children. It might be injured other people. Even animation programs are not good effect for children, because it containing violence action.

Then there are a lot of sexual scene in TV. In the U.S. there is a V-chip system because children can recive bad influence, but V-chip doesn't complete. Some people have not V-chip machine in their home, so their children might watch sexual TV programs. It is not good for children because there are problems that teenagers have sex early in the U.S. today.

Recently it is said that children's ability is decreasing because they watch TV and play TV games for a long time, so they don't study very hard. Long time ago, people read book more time than watch TV, but now most children don't read a lot of books. If they have free time, they watch TV. Children should read book and get much skill.

Now we generally have a TV and enjoy watching TV, but we have to be careful of TV because watching TV is sometimes bad, especially for children.

Student-Completed Checklist for a Cause and Effect Essay

CONTENT

GOOD　OK　NEEDS WORK

✓ ___ ___ The essay discusses a causal relationship between two items or concepts.

___ ✓ ___ The essay shows a direct link between the cause(s) and effect(s) with concrete examples.

✓ ___ ___ The essay makes a convincing link between cause(s) and effect(s).

___ ___ ✓ The essay uses "word pictures" to show the cause(s) and effect(s).

ORGANIZATION

GOOD　OK　NEEDS WORK

___ ✓ ___ The introductory paragraph leads to a thesis statement that indicates a direct link between stated cause and effect.

___ ✓ ___ Each paragraph in the body begins with a topic sentence.

___ ✓ ___ Each body paragraph shows a convincing relationship between cause and effect with specific details and support.

___ ___ ✓ The body paragraphs connect to each other with transition words or phrases.

___ ___ ✓ The concluding paragraph persuasively restates the thesis and summarizes the examples in the body paragraphs.

MECHANICS

YES　NO

✓ ___ Does each sentence have a subject, a verb, and a complete thought?

✓ ___ Does each sentence begin with a capital letter and end with a period?

___ ✓ Do all the word combinations (subject-verb, adjective-noun, noun-pronoun) agree with each other?

___ ✓ Does the verb tense express the appropriate time in each sentence?

___ ✓ Are all the words spelled correctly?

___ ✓ Are the articles (a, an, the) used correctly?

___ ✓ Are the forms of the words (verb, noun, adjective) used correctly?

✓ ___ Are all the word choices appropriate?

✓ ___ Are all the sentences in correct order?

REVISED DRAFT

Children Watching Television

Most people have television and love television shows. The shows give us a lot of information, fun things and sometimes serious things. Children especially love to watch television much of the time; however, watching television can be bad for them.

There are many violent television programs which are bad for children. For example, their favorite actors can kill a lot of people easily. They see the actors on different shows. Sometimes the actors die on one show, but they see them again on other shows and don't understand that to die is real. The actors are heroes for children, and children might imitate their actions on other children. Then the children can injure other people. Even animation programs do not have a good effect on children because they often contain violent actions. For example, animals or people hit other animals or people in cartoons.

There are also a lot of sexual scenes on television which are not good for children. Especially many movies on cable programs are supposed to be for adults only. In the United States there is a V-chip system because children can receive a bad influence from some shows. But the V-chip system doesn't work completely because some people do not have the V-chip machine in their homes, so their children can watch sexual programs. The sexual programs are not good for children because there are problems today when teenagers in the United States have sex early. Sometimes they have a baby or get a disease.

In addition to watching violent or sexual programs on television, children don't spend their time in a good way. Recently it was reported that children's ability is decreasing because they watch television and play TV games for a long time. Therefore, they don't study very hard or use their imagination. A long time ago, people read many books, for fun and for school, but now most children don't read a lot of books. If they have free time, they want to watch television.

Children need to read books to get good skills for learning and to enjoy their imagination.

Sometimes watching television is bad, especially for children. They can still enjoy watching television, but parents have to be careful about violent and sexual shows. Parents also have to be sure that their children do not spend a lot of time watching television.

6.6 Student Persuasion Essay

ROUGH DRAFT
Marriage for Females

Many people say what happiness of female is marriage and give birth. However, are those really make me happy in my life? Generally, those are happiness in females life, but those are accompanying with many problems such as (a) stress of bring up children, (2) take care of house and husband, (3) plus money probrem.

First of all, most females dream about bring up their children. However, that will be really hard and stressful because children have different personality and parents cannot control them even though when they are babys. However, parents have to teach them everything such as how to eat, speak, behave, and what is right or bad. Females have many time for have fun with their partner, friends, parents, and for doing their interests. Once they give birth, most their time have to use for their babys. Bringing up children is pleasure, but there are not only pleasure but also stressful, I believe, but females cannot lay it down.

Second of all, females have to take care of house and husband including bringing up her children at once. Commonly, male go to work, and earn money for his family. Therefore, houshold and take care of husband are wife's work. She have to clean up all their room, and do laundry. She also have to cook for her husband and children. In a case of have a husband who is unconcern she will have hard time. Most husband help his wife after work, but some of them never help their wife. If he says so, she have to do everything and maybe she will not have time to get some sleep.

Third, money probrem is most important part. Money makes people enrich, but especially people get marriage when they are still young, they will get trouble, and fight about money. Even if they are not too young, but a husband cannot make enough money to live. She will get stress about it. Maybe not only money but also other things because one of a stress will relate to different problem.

Finally, I do not have a dream about marriage. I really do not want to be bothered by a husband and money. When I get older I will think about get married. Conclusion, marriage life is not always make female happy.

Student-Completed Checklist
for a Persuasion Essay

CONTENT ─────────────────────────────

GOOD	OK	NEEDS WORK

✓ ___ ___ The essay states an opinion for a topic that usually evokes strong opinions.

✓ ___ ___ The essay provides clear, logical arguments for the stated opinion.

✓ ___ ___ The essay relies on concrete examples rather than on emotion.

✓ ___ ___ The essay forcefully states an opinion.

___ ✓ ___ The essay uses "word pictures" to show the examples.

ORGANIZATION ─────────────────────────

GOOD OK NEEDS WORK

✓ ___ ___ The introductory paragraph acknowledges that the topic can bring out an opinion quite contrary to the one in this essay.

___ ✓ ___ The thesis statement clearly states the opinion to be expressed in this essay.

___ ✓ ___ Each paragraph of the body begins with a topic sentence.

___ ✓ ___ Each of the body paragraphs provides clear reasons for the stated opinion.

___ ___ ✓ The body paragraphs connect to each other with transition words or phrases.

___ ___ ✓ The concluding paragraph restates the thesis and gives a summary of the essay's arguments.

MECHANICS ─────────────────────────────

YES NO

✓ ___ Does each sentence have a subject, a verb, and a complete thought?

✓ ___ Does each sentence begin with a capital letter and end with a period?

___ ✓ Do all the word combinations (subject-verb, adjective-noun, noun-pronoun) agree with each other?

___ ✓ Does the verb tense express the appropriate time in each sentence?

___ ✓ Are all the words spelled correctly?

___ ✓ Are the articles (*a, an, the*) used correctly?

___ ✓ Are the forms of the words (verb, noun, adjective) used correctly?

___ ✓ Are all the word choices appropriate?

✓ ___ Are all the sentences in correct order?

REVISED DRAFT
Marriage for Females

Many people say female happiness is marriage and giving birth. However, will those things really make me happy in my life? Generally, those things bring happiness to females' lives, but they are accompanied by many problems. The usual problems are the stress of bringing up children, taking care of a house and husband, and money problems.

First of all, bringing up children is often stressful. Most females dream about bringing up their children, but it will be really hard and stressful because children have different personalities and parents cannot control them even when they are babies. In addition, parents have to teach them everything, such as how to eat, speak, behave, and what is right or wrong. Married females might have much time to have fun with their partner, friends, parents, and for doing things they are interested in, but once they give birth, most of their time is used for their babies. Bringing up children is a pleasure, but it is also stressful, I believe, because females cannot ever leave this responsibility.

In addition to the children, females also have to take care of a house and husband at the same time. Commonly, a male goes to work and earns money for his family. Therefore, the household and care of the husband are the wife's work. She has to clean up all their rooms and do laundry. She also has to cook for her husband and children. In the case of having a husband who is unconcerned, she will have a hard time. Most husbands help their wife a little after work, but some of them never help their wife. If the wife has an unconcerned husband, she has to do everything, and maybe she will not have time to get some sleep.

A money problem is maybe more serious than the children or household problems. Money makes people enriched, but it causes problems, especially for people who get married when they are still young and do not have money in the bank or a good job. They will have trouble and fight about money. Even if they are not so young, many married people have money problems and very serious stress because not enough money is a problem for the children, the house, the food, everything.

In conclusion, married life does not always make a female happy. I do not have a dream about marriage because I really do not want to be bothered by a husband and money. When I get older, I will think very seriously before I get married.

6.7 Student Definition Essay

ROUGH DRAFT

Generation Gap

A generation is different between people's ages. A gap is a empty space. Everything has changed with each generation. Each generation has different opinions. Sometimes we have problems with our parents. This is called a "generation gap."

We have a different idea about work. They were born after world war II; therefore they were give hard time to live. For example, they could not eat enough, could not buy anything. My parents and their parents know what poor is, and they had to rebuild our country. As for me, I could eat anything I want. It is like opisite life. Maybe I do not know how important food is and I didn't appriciate for foods like my parents generation. I don't have to work for my food. My parents tell me to find a job after I graduate soon. Young people think if they don't know what kind of job they want, they can do a part-time job or just study something. The parents don't agree because it was natural for them to work after gradation when they were young.

We have a difference about music and hair color. In Japan most young people like better pop music than "Enka" because Enka is not exciting music for them. My parents tell me not change my hair color. They can't understand why young people do such brilliant colors, but for young people it is a part of fashions.

My generation think the important way is that men and women should be same, but my parents' generation think that is it important way that men have more effect to society than women. In fact there are more men than women in a government. My generation also has the important way that children shouldn't be grown by strict parents. Many of my parents' generation's people are very strict. Some of them hit their children when they teach manners or study and practicing sports. I think it is not good for children to grow.

Thus, each generation has different important ways. Each way has good points and weak point, but we have to recognize each other's ways. Maybe we and our children's generation is also so different.

Student-Completed Checklist for a Definition Essay

CONTENT

GOOD	OK	NEEDS WORK	
✓			The essay clarifies the meaning of a word or concept.
	✓		The essay shows that this word or concept is subject to different interpretations depending on different situations.
	✓		The essay clearly illustrates the interpretation of the word or concept in these different situations.
		✓	The essay uses "word pictures" to show the meanings of the word or concept in different situations.

ORGANIZATION

GOOD	OK	NEEDS WORK	
✓			The introductory paragraph leads to a thesis statement.
✓			The thesis statement declares what word or concept the essay will define.
	✓		Each paragraph in the body begins with a topic sentence.
	✓		Each body paragraph gives examples that show the meaning of the word or concept in different situations.
		✓	The body paragraphs connect to each other with transition words or phrases.
	✓		The concluding paragraph restates the thesis and summarizes the fact that the definition of the word or concept can vary according to different situations.

MECHANICS

YES	NO	
✓		Does each sentence have a subject, a verb, and a complete thought?
✓		Does each sentence begin with a capital letter and end with a period?
	✓	Do all the word combinations (subject-verb, adjective-noun, noun-pronoun) agree with each other?
	✓	Does the verb tense express the appropriate time in each sentence?
	✓	Are all the words spelled correctly?
	✓	Are the articles (a, an, the) used correctly?
✓		Are the forms of the words (verb, noun, adjective) used correctly?
	✓	Are all the word choices appropriate?
	✓	Are all the sentences in correct order?

Generation Gap

A generation is different between people's age levels, for example, child, parent, grandparent. A gap is an empty space without a connection. Each generation has different opinions, so we sometimes have a problem with our parents or grandparents when our opinions do not connect. This problem is called a "generation gap."

There is a "generation gap" in our different ideas about work. Our parents were born right after World War II; therefore they had a hard time living. For example, they could not eat enough, could not buy anything. They knew what "poor" is, and they had to rebuild our country. As for me, I can eat anything I want. It is like an opposite life. Maybe I do not know how important food is and I don't appreciate it like my parents' generation because I don't have to work for my food. My parents tell me to find a job soon after I graduate. I am like many young people because I don't know what kind of job I want, so I can have a part-time job or just study something. We have a "generation gap" because for my parents it was natural to work right after graduation when they were young.

We have another "generation gap" about music and hair color. In Japan most young people like better pop music better than "Enka" because Enka is not exciting music for them. Our parents heard only music from their country on the radio, but my generation can hear all the new music from every country in the world because of television, movies and the Internet. We also have a different opinion about what hair color should be. My parents tell me not to change my hair color. They can't understand why young people want such brilliant colors. They think I want to change myself when I do it. We have a "generation gap" because for young people it is not change; it is only a new fashion.

My parents' generation and mine have a big "generation gap" about women and strict parents. My generation thinks that men and women should be the same, but our parents think that it is more important for men to have more effect on society than women. In fact, there are more men than women in government and business, but it is changing a little. My generation also thinks children shouldn't be raised by strict parents. Many of my parents' generation are very strict. Some of them hit their children when they teach manners or study and practicing sports. I think it is not good for children to develop and this is a serious "generation gap" for us.

Thus, each generation has different ways and so we have a "generation gap." Each way has good points and weak points, but we have to recognize each others' ways. Maybe we and our children's generation will also be very different, and we will always have a "generation gap."

Answer Key

Unit 1

page 13
(Got It! Transitions)
   1. First
   2. and
   3. Even if
   4. therefore
   5. unless
   6. Furthermore
   7. because of
   8. if

Unit 3

page 46
(Got It! Parts of an Essay)
   1. introductory, first
   2. thesis statement
   3. three or more
   4. topic sentence (statement)
   5. concluding, final

Unit 4

page 60
(Got It! Introductory and
Concluding Paragraphs)
   1. The best introductory paragraph is **a.**

b is not a good choice because it begins with the specific thesis statement and then discusses more general ideas. An introductory paragraph, as you remember from previous units, should introduce and discuss general ideas and then narrow to a thesis statement.

c is not a good choice because there are too many details. This paragraph describes the subtopics of the thesis statement. That is what the essay body, not the introductory paragraph, should do.

   2. The best concluding paragraph is **b.**

a is not a good choice because the paragraph does not repeat the thesis statement in different words, nor does it summarize the supporting ideas of the essay. This paragraph has too many opinions and ideas.

c is not a possible choice because instead of summarizing, this paragraph repeats, in detail, all the information and examples from the body paragraphs. It is redundant.

page 70

(Got It! Sentence Order)

After the cheese on the top of the pizza is bubbling, it is time to take the pizza out of the oven. Slowly slide the pizza onto a cutting board. After you let it cool briefly, cut it into pieces with a pizza cutter. Do not cut the entire pizza before you begin to eat. Cutting it makes it get cold too fast, and cold pizza is not good. When everyone has been served, sit down with lots of napkins and a cool drink. Enjoy!

page 71

(Got It! Word Order in Individual Sentences)

1. How much rent can I afford each month?

2. The easiest place to look for homes is in the newspaper's classified section.

3. Ask the landlord or manager how old the place is and who lived there previously.

4. Once you have decided, you will need to sign a lease.

5. Always read the lease completely before you sign it.

Unit 5

page 128

(5.1 Sentence Fragments and Run-on Sentences)

Then it was off to the grocery store to pick up the cake. That added more stress. We picked up the cake and saw blonde bride and groom plastic figurines on the top. These blondes did not resemble my Korean fiancé or my Italian self. We took the cake to the restaurant where the reception was to be held the next day following the wedding. As I took it out of the car, the cake fell against the side of its box. Consequently, I had two blonde figurines standing on a dented wedding cake. The owner of the restaurant and I set the cake strategically on a table in the corner. The dented side was against a wall. Then I got out a marker and started coloring the figurines' heads. As luck would have it, the marker ran out of ink. The bride had a full head of new black hair and the groom had a head of two colors. I was tired. Tomorrow was my wedding day. Those figurines would provide entertainment, I decided, mistakenly thinking tomorrow would be a better day.

page 133
(5.2 Subject-Verb Agreement)
  1. is
  2. is
  3. Are
  4. lists, have to
  5. are, are

page 134
(Your Turn!)
  1. was, lives
  2. have, do, are
  3. has, is
  4. was, was, were
  5. appear, makes

page 135
(5.3 Verb Tenses)
  1. traveled, had planned, carried out, was looking/looked, thought, would be/was going to be
  2. stole, consumed, had intended
  3. regret, did not change, is, have ever seen

page 136
(Your Turn!)
  1. held, discovered, had stepped on
  2. was swimming, frightened, wished, had gone
  3. knew, would never marry, promised, lived

  4. realized, had told, would have given, have never lied
  5. were waiting, was playing, came, announced, had changed, would be

page 137
(5.4 Articles)
Once you have decided, you will need to sign **a** lease. **The** lease is **an** agreement between you and **the** owner. It is usually **a** one- or two-page document that lists all **the** rules both you and **the** owner have to follow. It will include information about **the** rent, **the** deposit, pets, utility payments, deposits for damages, and most importantly, **the** length of (**X**) time that you can live in **the** place.

page 139
(5.5 Adjectives: Active or Passive?)
An American foreign exchange student **studying** Portuguese in Brazil was having a weekly lesson with his Brazilian teacher. The teacher had just finished a long, **complicated** explanation of a grammar point, so she asked her student if he understood what she had just said . . . The American was **bewildered** . . . Body language, and particularly gestures, can be just as different from country to country as **spoken** languages, and more particularly, just as important.